BEST
CANADIAN
COVER LETTERS

by
Sharon Graham

Published By:

Career Professionals of Canada
Milton, ON Canada
866-896-8768
E-Mail: info@careerprocanada.ca
Internet: www.careerprocanada.ca

Sharon Graham, Author
Printed in Canada

Library and Archives Canada Cataloguing in Publication

Graham, Sharon
Best Canadian Cover Letters : 100+ best Canadian-format cover letters / Sharon Graham – 2nd Edition

Includes index.
ISBN 978-0-9880706-3-9

1. Cover letters–Canada. 2. Cover letters. I. Title.

HF5383.G728 2013   650.14'2   C2013-902196-5

DISCLAIMER

We have made every effort to provide complete and accurate information in this book. Still, it is possible that we have not found and corrected some typographical errors, omissions, or other mistakes. This book contains information that is current only up to its printing date. The sample cover letters included in this book have been edited from the original versions. Names have been fictionalized to protect the privacy of our clients and the organizations where they were employed.

This book does not provide legal or specialized counsel. Use the content as a general guideline and not the only source of your job search information. The author and the publisher will have neither liability nor responsibility to any person or entity with respect to any loss or damage caused, or alleged to have been caused, directly or indirectly, by the information contained in this book. If you require legal advice or other expert assistance, seek the services of a qualified professional.

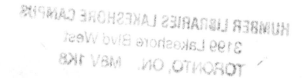

Table of Contents

Acknowledgements

To all the professional résumé writers who generously contributed their best Canadian cover letter samples for publication, I express my gratitude. You can see a complete contact list for these highly qualified professionals in Appendix B.

A special "thank-you" goes to Career Professionals of Canada's Certified Résumé Strategist Certification Committee for keeping me focused on continuously striving to learn and grow my own expertise in résumé and cover letter development. Thanks to Janet Barclay and Melanie Schlotter for your support.

I would like to express my appreciation to our clients who kindly agreed to allow us to publish their cover letters. Also, thank you to the hundreds and thousands of Canadians who have put their careers in the hands of professional résumé writers; you have enabled us to develop our abilities and talents as leaders in the Canadian Career Industry.

This book is dedicated to my dear husband, Wayne Graham, for his patience, love, and never-ending support, my parents for believing that I could achieve anything I set my sights upon, and Gracie and Kellie who gave me far too many happy puppy distractions throughout this project.

Most of all, thanks to God, who continues to make the impossible possible.

Sharon Graham
Canada's Career Strategist

Introduction

Every day, millions of Canadian job seekers participate in a tough competition in an attempt to reach their goal of getting an interview. Many apply haphazardly by flooding the market with a template résumé. Some however, employ a thoughtful approach using a cover letter and a strategic résumé. These professionals succeed in their job search by applying only to the most appropriate positions. They add a cover letter to their résumé to create rapport and interest in their background.

You can reap benefits and stand ahead of your competitors by submitting a well-written cover letter along with your résumé. This alone may be the reason you are selected over someone else who did not take the time to accompany his or her résumé with a cover letter.

This book is distinctively Canadian. The cover letter samples come from jobs and fields that exist across Canada. The book will provide you with the language, grammar, and style rules that you should apply within your cover letter. You will learn how Canadian standards and legislative requirements relate to the development of your letter. Finally, at the back of the book, we provide a number of resources to enable you to succeed in your job search.

Best Canadian Cover Letters is your one-of-a-kind resource. By leveraging the tools, information, and checklists provided and using it in conjunction with its companion book, *Best Canadian Résumés*, you will shine above your competition.

HOW THIS BOOK IS ORGANIZED

This book empowers you to create effective cover letters by taking you through a logical sequence of steps. The book is broken down into three main parts:

PART 1 PLANNING YOUR COVER LETTER

First-rate cover letter writing takes planning. This section will enable you to understand your job search goal. You will hone in on your target market, then match your pertinent qualifications to meet their needs. You'll learn how your Value Proposition can be propagated throughout the document to drive interest in your résumé and in you.

PART 2 WRITING YOUR COVER LETTER

Cover letter writing is a science and an art. This section discusses a variety of proven techniques used by professional résumé writers across Canada. You'll learn established structures and interesting methods of getting your message across in a concise and compelling way. By learning how to apply these guidelines, you will build a sound foundation to write an exemplary cover letter every time.

PART 3 SAMPLE COVER LETTERS

The largest portion of this book showcases cover letters that professional résumé writers have created for their Canadian clients. It includes some of the very best work produced by members of Career Professionals of Canada. All the samples are directly transferable to the Canadian employment market. These documents will provide you with inspiration to stimulate your thinking and creativity. A "strategic tip" box annotates each sample to help you visualize and understand how to apply a specific strategy.

Although it may be tempting to skip directly to the samples, you will find that using them in conjunction with the first two parts of this book will enable you to write a unique document rather than just a copy of someone else's work.

After reading this book, you will be fully prepared to launch an effective and successful work search armed with a strategy for developing effective cover letters for every situation. You'll be able to accompany your *Best Canadian Résumé* with a powerful marketing tool that will give you a distinct advantage in your job search.

PART 1
PLANNING YOUR
COVER LETTER

**1
Defining Your
Target Market**

Some job seekers mistakenly believe that if they create one "general" cover letter template, they'll be able to save time by blasting it everywhere along with their "general" résumé. With the belief that if one is good, then many must be better, they do not care who gets the documents or why. In fact, this poor tactic will hurt your chances of being viewed as a viable candidate for any position.

A better strategy is to develop a unique and thoughtful cover letter for each opportunity you encounter. You will be able to address the needs of your prospective employer and make a closer connection with them.

UNDERSTANDING YOUR GOAL

The goal of your cover letter is clear; you need to capture and fascinate the recruiter, employer, and other decision makers enough to make them want to learn more about you.

If your cover letter is to be successful, you need to:

- Create rapport and develop a personal connection with the reader.
- Draw in the reader to ensure a complete read-through of the entire cover letter.
- Entice every reader to want to take the next step and review your résumé in detail.
- Make your value seem so irresistible that the reader simply must call you.

FOCUSING IN ON YOUR TARGET

One well-written, targeted cover letter combined with an effective résumé is worth hundreds of résumés indiscriminately shipped out.

Your cover letter is a tool that supports your résumé and helps you to hone in further on your target market. Your résumé should already be clear about the kind of industry and job that fits you best. By focusing your cover letter further towards a specific position and company, you will develop a deeper connection with recruiters and employers reading your documents.

Your cover letter is a concise document that tells readers what you can do to address your prospective employer's needs. You have little space, but you need to advertise how your distinguishing factors will meet and exceed their requirements in a big way.

If you are going to make a good impression, you must tell employers what they need to hear. You can truthfully and succinctly discuss your offerings that are of value to them — but only if you are able to get into their heads and understand more about what they want to achieve.

The tighter your focus, the better the chances that the right people will see a good match. To save yourself time and energy, only select a few opportunities where you are a good fit and you can succeed. By narrowing your job search, you will better match yourself to appropriate roles. Remember, your goal is to enable the employer to see you as the ideal candidate for the job — not to send off hundreds of cover letters only to have them disappear into the black hole of the internet universe.

GATHERING INFORMATION ON YOUR TARGET

Your cover letter will command attention only if you have firmly established your understanding of the target. Make every effort to learn and know as much as you can about the employer and the job you are addressing. To do this, you must research every aspect that you can.

Most employers hire people to fulfil specific job requirements. So, before starting on your cover letter, do your research. Dedicate yourself to properly understanding the requirements of the position you are targeting. Investigate the company you are targeting as well. Only then will you be able to relate how your qualifications are a good fit. The more you know about the position, the company, and the decision makers, the more effectively you can communicate how you can help the employer.

It is best to have a different cover letter for each opportunity you encounter. Each focused letter is more likely to produce results in one situation, and less likely to work in others. This simply means that you will need to adjust your cover letter for each different role and company you target. In each case, instead of writing an open-ended cover letter that does not speak to the reader, tackle each individual decision maker's needs directly and candidly.

In Canada, we are fortunate to have numerous resources available to us. There are many ways to find out more about jobs, companies, and industries. Labour market information can be found in the online *Canadian Occupational Projection System (COPS)*. You can find links to key fields and their projections at the website for the *Alliance of Sector Councils*.

In addition to having the Internet at our fingertips, we can rely on many federal, provincial, and municipal government organizations. Programs offered by *Industry Canada* and *Human Resources and Skills Development Canada (HRSDC)* are available nationally. Additionally, you can find good information on your target market though regional and community-based resources across the country.

You can research your prospective employer and job online through their website. Additional information may also be found through the organization's marketing brochures, annual reports, and any other material you can get your hands on. However, the best way to learn about a company is by talking with people who are already employed there. Set up a brief meeting and perform an informational interview. Dig up as much as you can about the company, its product line, the services it offers, and the corporate culture. Find out what you can about the person to whom you are addressing your letter.

There are many other ways that you can find industry information. Start by looking at the websites of top companies and their competitors in the specific sector that interests you. You can also review professional, trade, and business association publications on the internet and in your local library. As any good researcher knows, speaking with people in the field will provide you with valuable information that you cannot get from online or printed documentation.

To sharpen your focus further, determine the requirements and responsibilities of the job you are targeting. Also, learn about the objectives and outcomes that the employer is expecting of the person who fills this position. You can uncover these things by studying job postings, but sometimes you can glean more by obtaining a copy of the full job description. Of course, it is best if you can schedule a discussion with a person who is working in the position. This way, you can uncover hidden details about what the company really wants but did not expressly outline in the job posting.

To learn more about researching your target market, refer to *Best Canadian Résumés*.

TARGET MARKET RESEARCH CHECKLIST

❑ I have narrowed my job search to a few good opportunities

❑ I have researched the specific position I am targeting (responsibilities/objectives)

❑ I have researched the specific company I am targeting (company, products, services, culture)

❑ I have studied the decision makers (recruiter, my supervisor, my team, my supervisor's manager)

**2
Clarifying Your
Value Proposition**

Your Value Proposition clearly tells the employer the reason why he or she should select you for the position. It answers the employer's question "Why Should I Hire You?" with a consistent response that runs like a thread through your cover letter, résumé, and interview.

The term "Value Proposition" comes from a marketing strategy. Companies create a sales pitch that clearly defines the value of the product that they sell to the buyers (their target market.) This is a very powerful concept that you can easily translate into your job search strategy — just think about yourself as the product and your next employer as the buyer.

Your own Value Proposition comprises three components: your employer's *buying motivators*, your *supporting qualifications*, and the *added value* you bring.

- *Buying motivators* are the reasons that an employer will want to hire someone; they are most often related to the "bottom line." Companies want people who can help them generate revenue, save money, and/or solve a problem. You need to show the employer what you have to offer that will help the company achieve its goals.

- *Supporting qualifications* are the credentials that validate your claim to resolve the employer's buying motivator. In other words, you need to show the employer proof supporting your statement using real-life examples from your background. All your qualifications related to the buying motivator you identified are important to mention in your Value Proposition.

- Your *added value* illustrates to the employer the special talents and contributions that you have to offer. It creates an image of you that is unique and valuable to the employer. Your *added value* shows that you bring much more to the role than what is merely expected.

If you have done your homework, your résumé already has a clear Value Proposition. Your goal now is to carry this message as a theme throughout your cover letter. Through it, you will be portraying your career brand.

Refer back to the top third of your résumé and highlight each component of your original Value Proposition. Determine the details and accomplishments throughout your résumé that directly relate to your Value Proposition. Once you have done this, you will be able to focus more deeply in your cover letter on your specific target employer's needs and wants.

Complete the following checklist to ensure that you have clarity in your Value Proposition. If you need help in defining it, refer to *Best Canadian Résumés*, which delves deeper into the construction of your Value Proposition.

MY VALUE PROPOSITION

❑   I know my employer's buying motivators

❑   I know my supporting qualifications that address the buying motivators

❑   I am clear about my added value and how it supports the buying motivators

3
Filtering Your
Qualifications

Before setting out to market yourself in a cover letter, you must be clear about the "product" you are promoting. You must have a strong understanding of yourself and your objectives. Only when you have an accurate picture of who you are in relation to what they are looking for, can you create a reason for the decision maker to pick up the phone and get in touch with you.

You can be assured that many of your competitors are listing their qualifications in their cover letter. To stand out from other candidates, your cover letter must not only reflect the exact qualifications your prospective employer is looking for, but it must also offer insight as to how you can exceed their needs. So take some time to figure out what you can offer that your next employer may see as a bonus.

SELECTING YOUR BEST QUALIFICATIONS

If you have done some initial self-assessment, you will have already uncovered a great range of qualifications. Your very first step in selecting the appropriate ones to feature in your cover letter is to compare the exhaustive list of education, experience, competencies, and accomplishments you possess against the requirements of the employer.

Before you start, gather all the documentation related to your qualifications, including your résumé, performance evaluations, salary reviews, awards, transcripts, personal biography, published articles and reviews, and letters of reference. Look through these documents and highlight only the strongest features that relate directly to your target job and employer.

You know all the broad aspects of expertise, background, and style that you have to offer. From these, select the *supporting qualifications* that best relate to the position. In addition, reflect on your *added value* — the unique offerings, special strengths, and additional features that will support your next employer's potential desires. With honesty and integrity, ensure that you address the employer's needs and wants while maintaining an accurate picture of yourself.

Here are some examples of features that may be valuable to highlight in your cover letter:

- If the position requires a higher level of education, consider including educational credentials, honours, and awards you received at school. Include your grade point average only if it is exceptionally high.

- If your previous employer(s) are in the same industry as your targeted employer, consider including company names, ranking, specialty, products, and services that may be applicable.

- If you know the specific objectives of the targeted role, consider listing your very best accomplishments that match those objectives. Include specific actions you took and the measurable results you achieved.

- If the position you are targeting requires specific expertise, consider listing the corresponding equipment, applications, and technical proficiencies you offer.

- If you have additional value that the employer may need, consider including those special features. Bilingualism in English and French, volunteer work in the sector, a feature in an industry publication, a special speaking engagement, a significant commendation, or a quote about you from someone important in your field might add value.

- If you have a distinctive style that is particularly important to the employer, consider discussing this aspect of your personality and individuality.

When it comes to your cover letter, you need to highlight only the best of the best. Only once you have a shortlist can you further eliminate the qualifications that are least valuable based on what you know about the job requirements and employer's expectations and desires.

Job seekers are often afraid of cutting out too many of their qualifications. In fact, this is a great strategy to strengthen your position. If you are diligent in slashing all items that are not the most important, you'll be left with a few gems. If you focus only on hard-hitting value, then every single word on your cover letter will count. This will allow you to present an extremely powerful message.

To learn more about how to uncover your qualifications, refer to *Best Canadian Résumés*.

TOP QUALIFICATIONS CHECKLIST (MATCH TO TARGET)

- ❑ Education (highest credentials, grades, honours, awards)
- ❑ Experience (connectable employers)
- ❑ Accomplishments (strongest actions, measurable results)
- ❑ Expertise (specific equipment, applications, technical proficiencies, specialty, level, prominence)
- ❑ Style (personality, individuality, dreams)
- ❑ Added Value (unique offerings, special strengths, additional features)

**PART 2
WRITING YOUR
COVER LETTER**

4
Understanding
Cover Letter
Anatomy

A strong cover letter is a critical component of your job search. It is all about attracting positive attention by making a great first impression. You have planned your approach carefully by focusing your target, clarifying your Value Proposition, and matching your supporting qualifications to your target's needs. Now, you are ready to develop a cover letter that concisely articulates all this information.

Your cover letter reveals clues to your level of professionalism. It demonstrates to your prospective employer that you can organize your thoughts and express yourself clearly. Make the effort to plan the structure of your letter carefully.

Your cover letter is usually the very first document a recruiter will see. A stunning cover letter is not just the introduction to your résumé — it is part of your complete presentation. If you present yourself well from start to end, you will not only make a powerful impression, but you will also show that you are worthy of the position and the salary they will be paying you.

ANATOMY OF A COVER LETTER

In Canada, a cover letter is typically one-page, but some organizations request further details, which may necessitate a lengthier document. Some sectors such as academic and government, and some jobs such as clinical researcher or board director, may characteristically require multi-page detailed cover letters.

A Canadian cover letter is not an autobiography. It is brief and to the point; in most cases, four to six paragraphs are sufficient. Your cover letter should demonstrate that you meet or exceed the requirements listed in the job description, and it should express your interest in the position. Any superfluous information will limit the chances of having your full submission read.

Your cover letter demonstrates to the prospective employer that you can express yourself in an organized and clear manner. The cover letter should be easy to scan with a logical progression.

If you're bewildered by how you're actually going to write a cover letter, it may help to break the letter down into its main components. Although there is no formula to writing a cover letter, in Canada, these components are used consistently in most letters:

- The letterhead
- The address block
- The opening
- The body
- The closing
- The signature block

We'll concentrate on just one component at a time. To be effective, you may need to adjust how you use and structure each part.

THE LETTERHEAD

For the best impact, mimic the header of your résumé in your cover letter. This will create a "branded" design through an upscale letterhead that matches the résumé. The look and feel of your complete package will present itself as if you are at the "top of your class."

As in your résumé, your letterhead must include appropriate contact information so that the reader is able to find you easily. Include your full name (with nickname, if appropriate), phone numbers including area codes, e-mail address, and any other pertinent contact details.

You may also want to include a headline or banner. An effective technique is to include a clever tagline or short phrase that concisely states your target job and/or Value Proposition.

THE ADDRESS BLOCK

The address block is the first portion of your cover letter tailored for the recipient of the letter. It is best to start the address block with a date line, which in Canada generally includes the month, day, and year in a structure like this:

January 1, 2014

Generally, it is best if your document does not look like a form letter that is being used for every application although, in Canada, we do have a number of scenarios where a form letter might be appropriate. If you are applying to labour-intensive positions where English writing skills are not a major requirement or if you have limited English language skills, you may prefer to have one well-prepared cover letter to use with each résumé you submit. If this is the case, you may use a "general" address block or omit portions of the address block. If you decide to use this strategy, you must still ensure that your content is targeted and delivers a strong Value Proposition.

There are other situations where you may need a more standard approach. For example, if you are handing out your résumé at a major trade show or job fair such as the annual National Job Fair and Training Expo in Toronto, you should already have researched companies you want to target. However, it would be prudent to bring a version of your cover letter that you can also distribute when you discover a new opportunity at the event.

From time to time, Canadian recruitment firms hold back the name of the hiring company when advertising a position. In those cases, it is perfectly acceptable to obtain the name of the primary recruiter working on the project and address the letter directly to the recruiter and his or her firm.

In Canada, the addressing portion of a letter is generally structured to include the recipient's full name, job title, company name, street address, city, province, and postal code. Here is an example of a typical addressing portion of a cover letter:

> Ms. Sharon Graham
> Executive Director
> Career Professionals of Canada
> 12-123 Any Street
> Milton, Ontario L1L 1L1

If you are applying to a particular job posting, it is beneficial to include a subject line below the recipient's address. This line would include the job title and/or reference number of the position that was advertised in a format similar to this:

> Re: Canada Post, Alberta Rural Mail Carrier, ARMC-014

Whenever possible, rather than starting with an impersonal "To whom it may concern" or "Dear Sir/Madam" address your letter to a specific person whenever that information is available. Here are some examples of salutations used in Canadian cover letters. Most cover letters start with a salutation like this:

- Dear Ms. Graham:
- Dear Mr. Graham,
- Dear Dr. Graham

Try to use politically correct language whenever possible. If you do not know the name of the person you are contacting, avoid terms such as "Dear Sir:"

- Consider something neutral such as "Dear Hiring Manager," "Dear Employer," or "Dear Human Resources Manager."
- If you know the name of the team filling this assignment, you may want to address the team e.g. "CEO Search Committee."
- If you know the title of the person to whom the open position reports to, you may want to address the title e.g. "Director of Sales and Marketing."

THE OPENING

The first paragraph of your cover letter is a vital lead-in to the rest of the document. This section must grab your targeted reader's attention and concisely show why you are the right person for the job. Refer to your Value Proposition and ensure that you answer the question: "Why should I hire you?" A well-written opening will draw the reader in and motivate him or her to read the rest of your cover letter.

Open your letter with a compelling sentence. From the very first line, you should be enticing your reader and stirring interest in you as the ideal candidate for the role.

The opening is a good opportunity to refer to the company by name and to state the title of the job you are targeting directly. In this portion of the letter, you may also want to state that there is an accompanying résumé.

Flatter the reader by discussing something you like about the company, the job, or their products and services. Build more rapport by showing the passion you have for this particular opportunity. You may do this by promising a benefit or identifying a timely solution to a current need.

THE BODY

In the body of the letter, tell the reader why they should select you instead of all the other qualified candidates. In two to four paragraphs, flesh out your Value Proposition and talk more about what you can do for the prospective employer than about what they can do for you.

You do not have much space in the body of the letter; so if you are having trouble condensing, you may want to select a few broad categories that best match your target employer's needs and wants. Then, write one paragraph outlining your best *supporting qualifications* for each category you selected.

To optimize space, you might want to use a bulleted list covering one of these items:

- Your strongest qualifications that match the job description.
- Most connectable, transferable achievements from your career.
- Key phrases that show competencies required for the job.
- Companies or projects that will impress and connect with the reader.
- Quotes from people who can attest to your performance in the job.

Don't forget to add tidbits to the body that will entice the reader further. For example, you may want to indicate your willingness to take a professional development program, travel, or relocate in exchange for the opportunity.

However you choose to structure the body of your letter, keep the content to a minimum. This way, you won't risk unnecessarily creating an additional page.

THE CLOSING

In your final paragraph, express your great interest in the company and thank the reader appropriately. Wrap your letter up with a call to action. Inform the reader regarding what future action you anticipate. Ask for an interview. Better yet, indicate to the reader when and how you will be following up with them — and hold up your end of the bargain.

THE SIGNATURE BLOCK

Your signature block will include space for your written signature before your printed name. You may want to include your formal credentials and job title if they add value to the overall letter. Since you will be including your résumé and other material in your document, you may also want to indicate that there is an enclosure at the bottom of the letter.

COVER LETTER STRUCTURE CHECKLIST

- ❑ The letterhead
- ❑ The address block
- ❑ The opening
- ❑ The body
- ❑ The closing
- ❑ The signature block

5
Employing Canadian Spelling & Grammar

This chapter reviews Canadian spelling and grammar outlined in Best Canadian Résumés, but it also provides additional points that you should consider carefully when writing your cover letter.

Canadian spelling and grammar is quite interesting and unique. This topic is important enough that it bears repeating the chapter in *Best Canadian Résumés* that discusses spelling and grammar in detail. However, cover letter writing is quite different from résumé writing.

By now, you are aware that the strategy and structure of both documents are dramatically different. There are also some important differences in how you use Canadian English in your cover letter versus the résumé.

In Canada, we find that the issue of "Canadian English" versus "American English" comes up regularly. Although Canadian English is not exactly the same as American English, it is not British English either. We employ subtle differences in spelling and grammar, which are unique to our country.

If a recruiter sees a glaring mistake, he or she may feel that you perform sloppy work and this could be just enough to eliminate you from the running. To pass the detailed review, your cover letter and your résumé must have no spelling or grammatical errors at all. This section explains how to ensure that your documents are impeccable.

SPELLING GUIDELINES

Canadian spelling is unique and takes on influences from our British and French ancestry, with a touch of Americanism. For example, in Canada, just as in the United Kingdom, we insert "u" in colour, favour, endeavour, and labour. On the other hand, we use "z" in organize and specialize, just as the Americans do. A hint of French comes out when we use "centre" instead of "center." Furthermore, instead of writing a "check" or collecting a "paycheck," we write a "cheque" and collect a "paycheque." A number of other Canadian words have idiosyncrasies; when in doubt, refer to the *Guide to Canadian English Usage* by Margery Fee and Janice McAlpine.

If you are using word processing software such as Microsoft Word, the system will likely default to the American language settings. If you do not use the appropriate language settings, the system will probably assume that you are spelling words correctly, even if they are wrong. So, before you start creating your cover letter, change your settings to Canadian English. This will ensure that the spelling and grammar you employ conforms to Canada's standards. Before completing your document, make sure to do a final spelling and grammar check. Readers who review your cover letter are not likely to find errors if you are thorough.

Don't rely solely on your computer to screen the spelling; you still must proofread your letter very carefully. Many Canadian words are spelled correctly when you mean to say one thing, but may be incorrect in another scenario. For example, you may want to list your "Class A drivers licence" in your cover letter to show your certification authorizing you to drive a tractor-trailer. This may "license" you (give you the permission) to drive the vehicle in Ontario. Note in the first sentence "licence" is a noun. In the second, "license" is a verb. Your computer would not be able to catch this difference, so you must be diligent in your proofreading.

You will find a list of commonly misspelled words in Appendix A. If you still are unsure of the spelling of a word, use a good Canadian dictionary such as the *Canadian Oxford Dictionary of Current English* by Katherine Barber to verify your work.

USING NUMBERS EFFECTIVELY

Using numbers in your cover letter can be tricky. In Canada, we generally spell out the numbers one through nine and write larger numbers as numerals. However, you may have used numerals throughout your résumé, since these characters tend to stand out while using less space. You may choose to use the correct grammatical structure (words and numerals) in your cover letter and use the more condensed numerals-only technique in your résumé. Whichever system you decide to use, stay consistent in each document. This will demonstrate that you purposely chose that particular structure.

In Canada, we use the dollar symbol, "$," to discuss currency in writing. There are many ways to highlight money in your cover letter. For example, you may choose to structure the figure as $1.5 million or you may choose to use $1.5 M. In both cases, since you are using the dollar symbol, you should not add the word "dollars" after the number; writing "$1.5M dollars" would be incorrect.

If you are discussing Canadian dollars in Canada, it is not necessary to point this out. For example, "$1.5 million CDN" would be inappropriate if all your values are Canadian. On the other hand, if you are discussing American dollars, then it is quite appropriate to use "$1.5 million U.S." or "$1.5 million USD" to let the reader know that the value is in a different currency.

When it comes to percentages, again, the choice is yours. Sometimes it is appropriate to use the word "percent" to define percentages in a cover letter, even if you have used the symbol "%" in your résumé. You never need to use both the symbol and the word together. For example, writing "10% percent" would be incorrect.

USING CAPITAL LETTERS CORRECTLY

We often use capital letters often in cover letters. Generally, use capital letters following Canadian style guidelines.

Capitalize the first letter of the main word for all titles and proper names used in your cover letter. Do not capitalize articles (a, an, the), conjunctions (and, but, or, nor, for, so), and short prepositions of four letters or less (at, by, in, on).

In your cover letter, you are likely to use capital letters in the following ways:

- Your headline (Highly Accomplished RCMP Officer)
- Your name (Jean Beaulieu)
- Your street addresses (123 Major Avenue)
- Company names throughout the letter (The Hudson's Bay Company)
- Your dates of employment (from January 2009 to date)
- Job titles that you are targeting (Accounting Manager)
- Geographical locations (Toronto, Ontario, Canada)
- Educational institutions (University of Toronto)
- Your credentials (Bachelor of Arts)
- Associations (Human Resources Professionals Association of Ontario)
- Formal program names (Human Resource Management Program)
- Formal names of courses you have taken (Accounting Principles)
- Books you have written (*Best Canadian Résumés*)
- Days that you work (from Monday to Friday)
- Holidays that you have worked (Canada Day)
- Adjectives related to nationality (French documentation)

The use of capitalization causes confusion for many. The consensus is that formal titles such as "Mayor Hazel McCallion" are capitalized but informal ones like "the mayor of Mississauga, Hazel McCallion" are not. In general, use the following structure for job titles: "my last position was director of services" or "I reported directly to the team leader Wayne Graham," or "professional singer Celine Dion attended the event." To highlight the position you are targeting use the formal name "I am a perfect match for your advertised position, Accounting Clerk."

Due to space limitations, you will be tempted to take advantage of acronyms, initials, and abbreviations in your cover letter. An "acronym" is a pronounceable word formed from the first letter or letters of a series of other words, such as ASCII (American Standard Code for Information Interchange). Conversely, "initials," such as HRPA (Human Resources Professional Association) are a group of first letters used to represent a name or expression. "Abbreviations" are short forms for words such as Alta. (Alberta).

If you are using an acronym, initial, or abbreviation that is not readily known by everyone in the industry where you are applying, it is best to spell out the word or phrase in full on first usage, followed by the short form in parentheses. Then, you can use the short form throughout the rest of the document. You don't necessarily need the short form if you do not use the word again in your cover letter.

In Canada, initials and abbreviations for academic degrees such as PhD, MBA, MA, MSc, BSc, BA, and BComm generally do not require periods, but if you decide to use periods, do it consistently. The abbreviations "Mr.," "Mrs.," and "Ms." take periods. Finally, the correct way to display "for example" in abbreviated format is "e.g." — not to be confused with "i.e.," the abbreviated form of "that is."

In most cases, it is not a good idea to use abbreviations such as Admin. (Administration), Prov. (Province), and Hi-Tech (High Technology) just to save space. You would be better off writing out the complete word within a proper sentence or bullet-point.

When it comes to Canadian provinces and territories, it is perfectly okay to use initials or abbreviations as long as you follow some specific rules. The following chart provides three variations. Stay consistent with the system you select throughout your cover letter.

PROVINCE OR TERRITORY	INITIALS	ABBREVIATION
Alberta	AB	Alta.
British Columbia	BC	B.C.
Manitoba	MB	Man.
New Brunswick	NB	N.B.
Newfoundland and Labrador	NL	N.L.
Northwest Territories	NT	N.W.T.
Nova Scotia	NS	N.S.
Nunavut	NU	Nun.
Ontario	ON	Ont.
Prince Edward Island	PE	P.E.I.
Québec	QC	Que.
Saskatchewan	SK	Sask.
Yukon Territory	YT	Y.T.

Refer to *The Canadian Dictionary of Abbreviations* by Thérèse Dobroslavic if you need to confirm the correct structure for English- and French-language acronyms, initials, and abbreviations commonly used in Canada.

USING PUNCTUATION CORRECTLY

In your cover letter, you must show a strong command of the English language. Use periods at the end of complete sentences, even if they are in bulleted lists. Use commas consistently — especially when you are listing a series of items. For example, if you decide to list "planning, forecasting, and budgeting" with a comma prior to the "and," use that structure throughout your cover letter. You can also use colons to introduce lists of items. Only use semi-colons to separate two main clauses if you need to distinguish each clause visually.

When incorporating quotations in a sentence, in Canada, we place the comma inside the quotes. When using parentheses (if we are to further clarify), the punctuation goes outside the final parenthesis. There is one exception: when you use a question mark or an exclamation point, place it inside the parentheses.

USING NON-SEXIST LANGUAGE

In Canada, the use of non-sexist language has become standard in formal communication. Always use good judgement and choose terms that are non-gender specific, whenever possible. Instead of "chairman," use "chairperson" or "chair." Instead of "manpower," consider "labour," "human resources," "staff," or "employees." We do not say "waiter" or "waitress," rather we refer to the person as a "server." Instead of "mailman" or "postman," you can try "mail carrier." Finally, rather than indicating "spokesman," try using the term "spokesperson."

Avoid using the masculine pronoun, "he" or "his" when referring to a person in general. For example, avoid a statement like this: "I trained and oriented each new employee, ensuring that he was quickly integrated in his role." Consider "I trained and oriented new employees, ensuring that each individual was quickly integrated into the position."

Only if you are referring to someone specific, should you use the correct pronoun that defines that person. For example, a comment like this would be appropriate in a cover letter: "I was recognized for taking the initiative to provide the senior accountant with administrative assistance during a busy tax season, which prompted an outstanding commendation from her."

THE INFLUENCE OF TECHNOLOGY ON CANADIAN ENGLISH

Modern technology and the speed of communication have influenced how we use language. If you are like many Canadians, you have been using the Internet in your job search. You may be using Twitter, texting, and chatting online to communicate with others. To get your message across, some words have been shortened and degraded somewhat to cram messages into short "chat" language. In addition to this, the Internet has exposed us to inconsistencies, differences, and mistakes from all over the world, making it more difficult to ensure correct use of language.

If you are discussing certain technological terms, you will need to make decisions on using capitalization and hyphenation. We tend to capitalize certain technology related terms such as Internet and Website, but this is changing as we see these words without capitalization just as often. Other words that refer to "electronic" terms, such as "e-mail," "e-commerce," "e-business," and "e-technology" may include the hyphen – or not. Whatever you do, employ consistency in your use of these types of terms.

Whether you are preparing a cover letter for the technology sector or want to show knowledge in certain hardware and software, it is important to know the correct capitalization for computer terminology. For example, many terms such as dBase, AutoCAD, and PowerPoint commonly use a mix of capital and lower case letters within the word.

Your cover letter should be a concise document, but it should also use proper spelling, grammar, and punctuation. Language is not static and the various iterations of the *Canadian Oxford Dictionary* are constantly evolving to incorporate changes and stay current. Ensure that you use a current version of the dictionary so that you are not bypassed for a simple error that could have been caught.

When it comes to language, some recruiters are becoming more tolerant, but you need to show that you have a strong command of English. If you are unsure of grammatical requirements, refer to a Canadian style handbook such as *The Canadian Press Style Book* by Patti Tasko. If you still decide to make an exception to a rule, be consistent throughout your document.

It goes without saying that you must have an outstanding cover letter. By paying meticulous attention to your letter, you will stand out and make a strong first impression, which will ultimately lead to a job offer.

**6
Writing
Strategically**

Just as your résumé is all about strategy, your cover letter is too. Strategic writing persuades the reader to pay special attention to your cover letter, your résumé, and — most importantly — to you.

Some people think that writing one version of your cover letter and copying that repeatedly is a great idea. You know better. You've already taken a powerful step by studying *Best Canadian Cover Letters*. Instead of cloning your letter, you are going to show your reader that you are hardworking, creative, and highly qualified for the job you are targeting.

Your goal is to capture and fascinate the recruiter, employer, or other decision maker enough to make them want to learn more about you. So, now you are ready to introduce yourself, present your Value Proposition, and get the reader to take action — all in one document.

STRATEGIC COVER LETTER WRITING

There is no formula to developing a strategic cover letter, but it is clear that you must flatter the recipient of the letter, present a persuasive sales pitch, and personalize the letter enough to express your individuality, personality, and style.

Your cover letter should be consistent with the résumé, but not repetitive. Since the letter accompanies your résumé, it is not necessary to regurgitate everything. Aim to mirror your Value Proposition in your cover letter, but make sure that you back up your claims with unique wording and examples.

If you decide to take content from your résumé, pull out and discuss only those parts that best match the requirements of the position. If you plan to highlight some selected achievements, cleverly modify the wording. Give the prospective employer a taste of what is to come, but avoid simply summarizing or copying directly from your résumé.

25

WRITE WITH INTEGRITY

When it comes to your career, your ethics and integrity are everything. In Canada, recruiters and employers perform reference checks regularly. When you act unethically, you will lose an opportunity, be found out on the job, or spend the rest of your career feeling guilty and unworthy.

There are many ways that you can express your authenticity, honesty, and morals through a cover letter:

- Never copy content directly from a colleague's résumé. Plagiarism is unethical and ineffective.
- Communicate your message with words that you commonly use. When you walk into that interview, your vocabulary, tone, and style must be appropriate and consistent with what you have put in your cover letter.
- Always choose to be truthful. One white lie can destroy your chances because most reputable organizations rigorously screen candidates.
- Never misrepresent yourself by overstating your experience or skills. Even if you do not have every qualification sought by the employer, stick to the facts.

Be true to yourself. By writing with integrity, you will position yourself to earn genuine credibility, trust, and respect from your next employer and all your colleagues.

SPEAK TO THE DECISION MAKER

You are likely to be addressing your cover letter to one reader. Speak to the person who will be receiving your letter. The person who reads your letter will be making a very important decision. You will either win or lose an opportunity to move forward based on the impression you make on this particular decision maker.

Here are some examples of decision makers who might be receiving your cover letter. Think about their needs carefully and adjust your content before addressing and sending the letter to them:

- The *contingency* recruiter works in an independent recruitment firm, but has no allegiance to you or any particular company. All this person wants to do is make a match between you and a job to receive a fee for this match. This type of recruiter generally has hundreds of cover letters and résumés in a database, so you'll need to make your cover letter rich in key words and key phrases so that your document can be found when they are looking for something in particular.
- The *retained* recruiter works in an independent recruitment firm, but has close ties to the hiring company. This recruiter has been selected by the company to find the right fit. It is likely that nobody else is aware of the position available and you'll need to dig to find out the name of the company in order to do your research for the cover letter.

- The *corporate* recruiter works within the company that you are targeting. This recruiter understands the company as an insider and may have developed the posting. If you know the job that you are going to target, you'll need to focus deeply on the job posting and the company needs.

- The *hiring manager* is likely going to be your prospective manager, supervisor, or team leader. This person knows the job inside out, but more importantly, since you will be working directly with him or her, personality and fit become extremely important. Your new boss wants to know that the two of you will get along and that you will coexist nicely within the team structure.

You may be addressing your cover letter to someone else in your network of contacts such as the head of the company, a team member, or a person who can offer you "a way in" to a particular job. No matter whom you are sending your letter to, always consider and address the needs and motivation of that person before finalizing your cover letter.

ENCOURAGE READABILITY

An effective cover letter is easy to read from style and formatting perspectives. Bunched up text and long paragraphs frustrate recruiters who have to review many cover letters and résumés on an ongoing basis.

Since the cover letter is a marketing document, first impressions count. The first time a recruiter sees your document, he or she will probably scan it briefly. If your letter does not look professional and appealing, the reader will pass it up. A thoughtfully designed cover letter that takes advantage of creative elements will differentiate you from the rest and it will encourage the reader to go through the document.

Your cover letter must speak to your target market's requirements. Centre it on their needs – not your wants. Do not use the pronouns "I" or "me" excessively. Talk more about what you can do for the prospective employer than about what they can do for you.

Cut to the chase. Employ the concept of "fat-free" writing. Avoid superlatives and eliminate all non-essential language. Don't overstate or use too many qualifiers, just state the facts cleanly and clearly. This will help you feature the most pertinent information for the reader.

Make your document irresistible by using future-focused wording. Don't simply summarize what you have done, but discuss what you can do in the future. Give the decision maker a taste of what is to come if they select you. Make sure that you back up your claims with specific examples of your proven achievements that demonstrate the results you offer that will be meaningful to them in their search for the right candidate.

Use words that make sense and are easily understandable to the reader. Stay away from acronyms, initials, and abbreviations unless you are certain that the reader will know those terms.

You can strategically make your cover letter more readable by using active language rather than passive language. For example, instead of saying "the project was completed by my team" say "My team completed the project."

Ensure that all the spelling, grammar, and mechanics are impeccable. Check and recheck the cover letter for typos and other errors. Once you have created your cover letter, read your document aloud and make sure that everything flows the way it should. To be extra certain that you are on the right track, make sure to get the opinion of a trusted professional. Have someone qualified proofread and edit your cover letter to ensure that there are no errors at all.

DEAL WITH OBSTACLES

Everyone has challenges in their career and life that they must mitigate in their job search. Some people are starting out in their career and have no work experience. Some are new immigrants looking for their first job in Canada. Others are transitioning out of one role into another where they have little or no background. Still others are coming back to work after a long leave of absence. Whatever obstacles or barriers you have, you must deal with them effectively.

The general guideline is to avoid discussing any factors that might exclude you. In most cases, it is best not to include any references to career or personal issues because you may bring up a concern that is not overtly evident. However, sometimes the challenge is so glaring that you must address it in your cover letter in order to get past the decision maker. In addition, it is in your best interest to plan and practice your delivery of a message to mitigate the obstacle during an interview.

Here are some common obstacles and barriers and how you can address them in your cover letter — if you must talk about them at all:

- *You have a disability* — in Canada, many ethical companies will find a way to accommodate the disability. Still, you will need to weigh the "pros and cons" of disclosing your disability on your cover letter. You do not need to mention anything (visible or invisible), if it will not affect your job performance. However, if your disability is going to be immediately recognized as soon as you attend the interview, it is generally best to address it in the cover letter. Do not surprise the interviewer or anyone else; let them know so that they can prepare and do what it takes to accommodate you.

- *You are a new immigrant* — if you have no Canadian experience, you may encounter challenges. However, increased globalization has made it easier for highly qualified new immigrants to express their valuable skills and international experience. So, if you are a skilled worker and you are targeting a similar position to the one you left in your country, then focus on the powerful things you achieved in your role.

- *You have been terminated* — generally, in Canada, we do not discuss the reason for leaving a position in a cover letter. If you must, focus on all the good things that you accomplished during your tenure. Do not say anything negative about your employment situation or your life in general. Your reason for termination is best delivered in person so that your personality and humanity can counter any potential employer's concerns.

- *There are gaps in your employment* — if you have a glaring gap in your résumé and you are compelled to explain it, then discuss it briefly in the cover letter and move on to the topic of how you will help them. Show that you did something worthwhile during the gap. Discuss something that added positive value during the time that you were not working.

- *You have a short employment term* — explain why you left the job in the best way possible — either because you wanted to find a better fit, focus on your long-term career goal, finished the project earlier than scheduled, or successfully completed a contract assignment.

- *Your education is incomplete* — the best way to deal with this is to focus on your strong experience. Only indicate that you started on a required credential if you are planning to complete it or if you were recruited into a dream position that you just had to take.

- *You have no education* — talk about the fact that you are a hard worker who made a proactive choice to get right into your first job. If you mastered the trade "on the job," say so. Mention your interest in ongoing professional development and upgrading of your skills if that is true.

- *You have no experience* — if you have limited employment experience, beef up your cover letter with many accomplishments from your background that are transferable into the role you are targeting. If you have no employment at all, draw out these achievements from your educational, personal, and volunteer successes.

- *You are an older worker* — discuss only your last ten years of experience. Emphasize a number of the amazing accomplishments you attained in your career. Remind the reader that the deep expertise you bring to the table is extremely valuable.

Avoid providing a salary history or salary expectations in your cover letter. This kind of information is more likely to cost you a job than not. If the job ad says that you will not be considered if you do not provide the details, give a historical salary range and state that your salary requirements are flexible.

TAKE ADVANTAGE OF CANADIAN LEGISLATION

Canadian human rights legislation guards against discrimination by strictly forbidding recruiters and employers to ask for certain personal information. Companies are not allowed make employment decisions based on attributes other than a person's qualifications to perform a job. Therefore, it is not necessary for you to include your age, sexual, political, or religious orientation, marital status, health, or race in your cover letter.

In addition, for your own protection, it is advisable that you never give out personal information such as bank account numbers, social insurance numbers, or credit card numbers. Laws vary by province and territory. When in doubt about what to include, check with the *Human Rights Commission*.

FOLLOW THE EMPLOYER'S LEAD

When submitting your finalized cover letter and résumé, do it in the way that the employer wants to receive it. Most Canadian employers accept applications submitted by e-mail or on their website, but some still do not.

Cater to your recruiter's preference. If he or she requests a résumé in hardcopy or by facsimile, send both the cover letter and the résumé that way. When you are printing and mailing your document, select a high quality white or off-white résumé stock. If you are faxing it, use black print on plain white paper. Don't forget to sign your cover letter.

Regional *Community Access Point (CAP)* programs, libraries, and schools provide computers, faxes, printers, and paper to enable you to write a compelling cover letter. You'll also be able to e-mail your letter and résumé through these resources.

Keep copies of your cover letters easily accessible. Log how and when your letters were sent so that you can follow up on them and retrieve them when your prospective employer calls.

These days, many cover letters and résumés employ colour as a distinguishing strategy. Many of the samples presented in this book were originally designed in colour. You can see colour samples online at http://www.SharonGraham.ca.

COVER LETTER STRATEGY CHECKLIST

- ❑ Does not directly repeat content from the résumé
- ❑ Is written with authenticity, ethics, and integrity
- ❑ Focuses on the needs and motivation of the decision maker
- ❑ Uses techniques to encourage readability
- ❑ Deals effectively with all challenges and obstacles
- ❑ Is compliant with Canadian legislation
- ❑ Follows the employer's lead

PART 3
SAMPLE
DOCUMENTS

7
Best
Cover Letter
Samples

Entry-Level
New Graduate & Trades

Cover Letter Strategist: Lynda Reeves

KATE BELLERA, BEng.

123 Any Avenue
Hay River, NT • X1X 1X1
(867) 555-1234 • kbellera@careerprocanada.ca

June 15, 2013

Mr. John Smith
President & COO
ABC Company
123 Main Street
Hay River, NT X1X 1X1

Dear Mr. Smith:

Mr. Smith, I was speaking recently with your colleague, John Power, who mentioned that your firm is in need of a reliable professional capable of delivering accurate administrative assistance. In my accompanying résumé, there is verifiable information concerning my ingenuity, efficiency, and accuracy with regard to all aspects of my work performance. I'm a dedicated customer service provider with excellent computer and data management skills. I can be counted on to meet and exceed deadlines, even while juggling a number of tasks at one time.

Prior employers have been impressed with the precision and problem-solving style that I apply to every situation. I have solved numerous concerns, from time planning to process improvement needs. Focused on the end result, I am proficient at researching solutions on the web and in relevant reports and publications.

My technical and service orientation would serve your busy enterprise well. I possess a positive, calm demeanour, which is reassuring to peers and clients alike. These features are enhanced by my complete involvement with, and support for, team and business objectives.

In one company in particular, I was responsible for meeting challenges where there were communication and training issues for personnel with a limited foundation in English. Through a tenacious, careful approach, and active involvement of all employees, I designed manuals and created laboratory-testing records, which incorporated simple points and logical flow. These projects resulted in forms that were valued tools for both staff and management.

In 2009, I completed my Bachelor in Engineering degree. I am proud of this achievement, not only for the education I gained, but also because I followed through on this with determination and perseverance. I have since recognized that my talents for observation, creativity, and detail would be better applied in more direct customer interaction and administrative situations.

Mr. Smith, I am able to accept a permanent, full-time position starting immediately and would welcome the opportunity of a personal interview. I can be reached at your convenience at the number above or by email. I will make a follow-up call in a week to ensure you have had an opportunity to review my résumé. Your time and consideration of this is appreciated.

Sincerely,

Kate Bellera

Enc. Résumé

Administrative Assistant. The lead-in to this letter identifies a colleague who has referred the candidate to the firm. This technique leverages the mutual acquaintance for that all-important interview.

SARAH GREEN

PROJECT ASSISTANT

123 Any Street, Suite 100
Markham, Ontario L1L 1L1
sarahgreen@careerprocanada.ca
647-555-1234

February 21st, 2014

Ann's Advertising Studios
123 People Drive, Studio 1
Markham, Ontario L7L 1L1

Reference: Project Assistant

Dear Selection Committee:

The key to creating a strong team is to set a common goal. The attributes of a project assistant that Ann's Advertising Studios needs are in sync with my own characteristics, which will embody the answers to the following three small questions:

Who are you? I am an organized and self-motivated project assistant.
What do you do? I provide creative, insightful, innovative, and strategic support to your team.
Why does it matter? Adding the most value to your team is the best choice you can make.

As a recent graduate from the Business Administration Marketing program at Georgian College, I offer a solid foundation for joining your organization as a project assistant. This includes a unique mix of education and work experience. Academically, my multifold course work allowed me to learn to deal with circumstances effectively and efficiently. Through my outstanding grades, I demonstrated the ability to manage and accomplish multiple simultaneous tasks independently and as part of a team in a fast-paced, high-pressure, deadline-driven environment.

My experience as a marketing and administrative assistant in three different workplaces gives me the skills necessary to perform various tasks required of an excellent project, account, and administrative employee. I am able to work in a Macintosh environment to create brochures, press releases, and flyers using Adobe Photoshop, Adobe Illustrator, and QuarkXPress. Moreover, I have hands-on experience using social media intelligence to improve and maintain long-term impact on businesses and brands.

Co-operative education experience helped me gain knowledge in general clerical and administrative support; I monitored phones and e-mails, performed routine office duties, and executed numerous tasks that involved computer programs using the Microsoft Office Suite. I pay close attention to details and ensure that work is of the highest quality and error-free. My ability to measure customer needs, analyze market trends, and resolve problems guarantees high customer service by maintaining positive relationships with current and potential clients.

I am confident that I will make a valuable contribution and a positive impact as a project assistant on your team by applying my strong motivation and professional skills. My salary expectation would be consistent with my education and work experience in the industry. My résumé is enclosed for your consideration and I would be grateful for an interview. Please do not hesitate to call me.

Sincerely,

Sarah Green

Advertising Project Assistant. The lead-in to this letter captures immediate attention. With three small questions, the candidate clearly shows a match to the targeted position.

Cover Letter Strategist: Lynda Reeves

TAYLOR RED
123 Any Avenue • Saskatoon • Saskatchewan • S1S 1S1
(Home) 306.555.1234 • tred@careerprocanada.ca

June 1, 2013

Martinsville Animal Control Agency
123 Main Street
Martinsville, Saskatchewan S1S 1S1

Re: Dispatcher for Animal Control Officers

I am writing in response to your ad in the Saskatoon Phoenix News for a dispatcher to the animal control officers in your company.

My background is a diverse one, which includes many roles as an exceptional client service representative. You will find me to be an enthusiastic, understanding person who enjoys many challenges. For many years, I have watched documentaries depicting the tragic situations or deplorable conditions in which animal control professionals have discovered animals. It would be an honour to work for an organization that performs such necessary rescues and works with our Humane Society to further awareness of the plight of so many creatures.

My personal and work experiences have showcased my excellent organizational skills. I am a proactive and engaged team player, able to focus on goals and set priorities. Clientele and colleagues alike have commented upon my calm demeanour and tact in defusing sensitive situations. Whether dealing with animals (my own or others) or with people, this latter capability has proven valuable in many situations.

After purchasing a PC and teaching myself Internet searching, e-mail systems and word-processing, I have discovered an aptitude for computer technology. I'm known for my ability to quickly assimilate new accountabilities, and noticed for my accuracy and attention to detail.

With my love and respect for animals, being associated with the Animal Control agency in any capacity would be welcome. I am confident that my experiences and abilities, combined with my enthusiasm, will serve your firm well. I look forward to meeting with you at a mutually convenient time to further discuss my qualifications.

Sincerely,

Taylor Red
Encl.

Animal Control Dispatcher. In paragraph two, this candidate displays her interest in animal rights and animal control, while concurrently demonstrating her respect for the organization and its work.

EMILY TOTTENHAM, M.Sc.

123 Any Avenue
Kitchener ON N1N 1N1
519.555.1234
emilyt@CareerProCanada.ca

FORENSIC PSYCHOLOGIST

July 16, 2013

Mr. John Smith, HR Manager
Corrections Canada
123 Main Street
Toronto ON M1M 1M1

Re: Assistant Researcher

Dear Mr. Smith:

After completing a B.Sc. in Psychology at the University of Western Ontario, I went on to complete a Master's at the University of Kent, U.K. With hard work and determination, I undertook a full course load and dissertation over one year, and graduated with "distinction," the highest honour given in the U.K. This accomplishment displays the energy, enthusiasm, commitment and work ethic that I bring to work and study. Looking to make a meaningful contribution, I submit my curriculum vitae in application for the position of Assistant Researcher with Corrections Canada.

I specialized in Forensic Psychology and am especially keen on conducting research in this area, and have learned through experience that my skills and personality are very well suited for this role. In the three Research Assistant positions I have held, I have displayed exceptional thoroughness in all details including studying relevant research literature, programming of instrumentation, and extensive piloting prior to the rollout of a study to ensure a smooth transition from theory into practice.

Colleagues have noted the ease with which I am able to address complicated data analysis; my sound judgment results in safe, well-tended participants; and my interpersonal skills contribute to a friendly, collaborative team atmosphere. In addition, I am both a critical and creative thinker, able to conceive new studies to further advancements in forensic psychology.

Strong communication skills, which enhance the work environment and facilitate the writing of related papers for publication, strong organizational and time management skills, and a highly disciplined nature further round out my contributions.

I welcome the opportunity to meet with you in person, and do hope to hear from you with an invitation to an interview. I thank you for the consideration.

Kind regards,

Emily Tottenham
Att: 2 pages

Assistant Researcher. This candidate expertly transitions her post-graduate work experience in the U.K. back to Canada. After the opening, she dedicates the rest of the letter to her experience and skills rather than focusing on the location.

COURTNEY TRAIN

123 ANY AVENUE, APT. 100
TORONTO, ONTARIO
M1M 1M1

TEL: (416) 555-1234

Bartender / Server

For: A nightclub or hospitality establishment

Please consider this letter of introduction as an expression of my interest in exploring employment opportunities with your organization. I have attached my résumé for your review, citing a detailed overview of my strengths including customer service and my ability to communicate well with the public and staff members.

I believe I can add value as a team member and perform my responsibilities in a professional and timely manner. My experience consists of the ability to prepare accurately measured cocktails, hands-on expertise with the Pro Bar System, knowledge of domestic and imported beers, and the ability to match the type of drink with the type of glass used.

Ultimately, I firmly believe that I am a candidate whom you can come to depend on. I have much to offer and feel that I will benefit a company where I can make a significant work ethic contribution to profits as a resourceful and results-oriented individual. My goal is to work full time on a long-term basis. To date, I have worked in smaller establishments and, at this time, nothing would please me more than to join a larger team of people as I move forward in my working experience.

I very much look forward to hearing from you so that we can schedule an interview to talk about your expectations and the possibility that my abilities are similar to those you are currently seeking to fulfill.

Yours very truly,

Courtney Train

Attachment: Résumé

Bartender. This interesting approach does not include any recipient addressing information. As a result, the candidate can easily drop off a copy of the letter and résumé at various nightclubs, bars, pubs, and other locations in one swift run.

Sally Sheridan

123 Any Avenue, Prince George, BC, V1V 1V1
Home Phone: (604) 555-1234 • Cell Phone: (604) 555-2345
Email: sally_sheridan@CareerProCanada.ca

August 13, 2013

Jane Smith
Hiring Manager
ABC and Associates Inc.
123 Main Street
Prince George, BC V1V 1V1

Dear Ms. Smith,

Re: Expression of Interest – Bookkeeping Growth Position

After more than 16 years of experience, I am seeking an opportunity to apply my professional training by transitioning my career as a Financial Services Assistant into bookkeeping. I believe that the reputation for integrity and reliability that ABC and Associates has built is something with which I would like to align my career as a bookkeeper.

I am interested in offering my expertise as a Bookkeeper Trainee at a junior administrative pay level, leveraging my experience as a senior administrative assistant, office manager, and business process innovator.

As an employee, I am able to offer ABC and Associates:

- ✓ A savings in salary and overtime dollars by taking on extra bookkeeping tasks in addition to full-time senior administrative duties, at a junior pay level.

- ✓ A proven ability to decrease organizational paper burden and increase business process efficiency.

- ✓ An educational background in bookkeeping, income tax preparation, and experience performing complex accounting functions.

- ✓ A flexible and dedicated worker who learns quickly and works hard to ensure organizational success.

I will contact your office to follow up with you on August 20th, 2013. I would be pleased to set a time for a suitability interview with you at that time to further review my qualifications, and the benefits your organization could realize by hiring me. Please feel free to contact me prior to August 20th if you have any questions.

Sincerely,

Sally Sheridan

Bookkeeper. This career-changer's "hook" is that she is willing to perform administrative duties and receive junior administrative pay in exchange for a developmental bookkeeping position.

Cover Letter Strategist: Stephanie Clark

LAURA MULMAN

123 Any Avenue · Kitchener ON · N1N 1N1 · 519.555.1234 · lauram@CareerProCanada.ca

July 16, 2013

Mr. John Smith, Recruiter
Public Service Commission of Canada
123 Main Street
Waterloo, Ontario N1N 1N1

Re: **Border Services Officer**
Reference Number: BSF07J-008731-000006
Selection Process Number: 08-BSF-EA-NBSO-0033

Dear Mr. Smith:

I believe that my unique mix of education and work experience established a solid foundation for joining the Public Service Commission of Canada as a Border Services Officer, and for effectively furthering the goals of Canada's Border Services Agency.

I have recently graduated with an Honours Bachelor degree, where my studies focused on an investigation of cross-cultural political and religious practices. These studies not only provided insight into global differences in approach, but also explored commonalities and served to continue developing my appreciation of human diversity.

Throughout university I worked at a local Urgent Care Medical Clinic. Given that Waterloo Region is undeniably under-serviced as far as family physician care is concerned, the clinic is extremely busy, and easily half of its clientele consists of new Canadians. The five years working at the clinic provided me the opportunity to deal with:

- pressure on a regular basis, and developing a measured response;
- crisis situations, which developed my ability to stay calm in the midst of chaos;
- assessing legal paperwork and communicating its repercussions to patients; and
- non-English speaking clientele further developing my communication strategies.

I welcome the opportunity to meet the criteria and conditions of employment for this position, and look forward to receiving a favourable response from Canada's Border Services Agency to proceed with the next step in the process towards becoming a Border Services Officer.

Sincerely,

Laura Mulman
Att: 2 pages, résumé

PROFESSIONAL   DIPLOMATIC COMMUNICATOR   DEPENDABLE

Border Services Officer. This recent graduate knows how to follow rules. She includes the job title and all known reference numbers in the address block to ensure that the recipient does not misplace this cover letter.

JOSEPH COHEN

123 ANY AVENUE, OTTAWA, ONTARIO, K1K 1K1

Cell: 613-555-1234

Email: busdriver123@CareerProCanada.ca

June 9, 2013

Toronto Transit Commission
Human Resources Services
123 Main Street
Toronto, Ontario M1M 1M1

Dear Hiring Manager

RE: TRANSPORTATION OPERATOR – Bus Driver

Please consider this letter of introduction as an expression of my interest in exploring employment opportunities with the Toronto Transit Commission (TTC). I have attached my résumé for your review citing strengths including my ability to deliver high quality customer service.

I meet all your qualifications as outlined on your website and am a competent team member and leader. At this time in my career, I am ready and eager to take on a different challenge and know that my transferable skills would enable me to adapt quickly.

Ultimately, I firmly believe that I am a candidate whom you can quickly come to depend on. Image is very important to the TTC and I will ensure that my image and alertness to safety is one of first-class. I will operate each vehicle responsibly, as I have a clean driving record in good standing and have good knowledge of streets and intersections, and highways.

I add value on a continual basis and perform my responsibilities in a professional and timely manner. At this time, I would very much like to join your team as a bus driver and make a positive difference with an upbeat friendly attitude. With a career path in health and safety inspection, and maintenance, I will already bring great value. In time, after having proven myself, I am certain that you will consider moving me up the ranks in the transportation division towards my long-term goal of becoming a transportation safety officer.

I look forward to an interview to elaborate further and find out how I can fulfill your expectations as a mature employee with excellence in transportation, safety, and maintenance.

Yours very truly,

Joseph Cohen
Résumé – 2 pages attached

Bus Driver. This individual strengthens his application by focusing the letter on transferable skills from his previous positions in health and safety, inspection, and maintenance.

Cover Letter Strategist: Brenda Collard-Mills

Carol Cochrane, MSW, BA

linkedin.com/in/infocarolcochrane

Toronto, Ontario | M1M 1M1 | Phone: 647.555.1234 | Email: carolcochrane@careerprocanada.ca

Envisions an integrated society where all individuals are valued

January 12, 2014

Ms. Tracy Smith
Human Resources Manager
YYZ Community Health Services
4567 Adelaide Street
Toronto, Ontario M1M 1M1

Dear Ms. Smith:

My résumé in application of the Community Social Worker position, as posted on your website, is enclosed for your review. I launched my career with a diploma as a Developmental Service Worker, further advanced my academic background by earning a B.A. in Social Development Studies, and am excited about my upcoming graduation from Wilfrid Laurier University with a Master of Social Work. With my current academic goals accomplished, I am eager to once again make a significant and dedicated contribution within the health care community.

You serve a diverse demographic comprising struggling new immigrants in a high crime environment, along with an aboriginal component. My recent placements in the low income, multi-cultural Lakeshore West and South GTA regions have prepared me well to support your objectives. Allow me to expand by providing a brief synopsis of my involvement in these areas.

In two three-month placements with the Ministry of Community and Social Services and the Ministry of Child and Youth Services, I worked on the Development Services Portfolio, heightened industry awareness of the unique needs of an aboriginal community, and served on numerous appointments pertaining to Violence Against Women. As one of ten graduate students teaching weekly post-secondary classes to female inmates, I have expanded my understanding and empathy for people incarcerated in a federal prison.

My earlier seven-month placement was at St. Margaret's Foundation, a non-profit agency serving the southern Toronto integrated community for 100 years. I wrote a Newcomer Settlement Program Manual, developed a tax workshop for new immigrants, and elevated my social services and community agency knowledge by participating on a multitude of multi-agency committees and working groups.

Prior to pursuing my Masters degree, I held a variety of positions assisting youth and adults facing various challenges to integrate and achieve success in our educational and societal systems.

I truly care about making a positive impact in the lives of the clients I serve, embrace challenges for the opportunities they present, and have developed a reputation for my ability to quickly jump into and assess a situation, extrapolate pertinent information, and formulate a comprehensive care plan.

I relish the opportunity to meet your interview team to further substantiate the value I can bring to YYZ Community Health Services upon my appointment. Thank you for your consideration. I anxiously await your call.

Sincerely,

Carol Cochrane

Community Social Worker. After completing her Masters of Social Work degree, this student is ready to penetrate the market. She provides a synopsis of current, pertinent professional experience gained during practicum placements.

Marie-Isabelle Arsenault

819.555.1234 ▸ www.linkedin.com/in/infoisabellea ▸ isabellea@careerprocanada.ca

BILINGUAL INSIDE SALES & CUSTOMER SUPPORT PROFESSIONAL

CLIENT SERVICE REPRESENTATIVE | REPRÉSENTANTE AU SERVICE À LA CLIENTÈLE

21/8/2014

Ms. Jane Smith
Staffing Consultant
ABC Recruiters
Ottawa, ON CANADA K1K 1K1

Re: Customer Service Administrator, Best Technology Company (Job Posting 123-4)

Dear Ms. Smith,

When sourcing and hiring candidates, ABC Recruiters looks for ethics and quality service – and these are the attributes I offer your client, Best Technology Company. You will want to interview me because I have all of the competencies required for your advertised position of Customer Service Administrator: client service excellence, technical sales support experience, and fluency in English and French.

Best Technology Company is known for its outstanding business practices, built on the founding principles of inclusion and integrity. You may have noticed on my résumé that I was on sabbatical for two years, which I will explain with complete transparency: I have fully recuperated from an automobile accident, where I was a victim of a drunk driving incident. Although I now use a wheelchair, I am fully equipped to satisfy all the responsibilities of the Customer Service Administrator role.

An optimistic and practical professional, during my rehabilitation period, I proactively completed the Contact Centre Operations Certificate offered through Service Training Centre. I also offer proven strengths acquired in my previous retail sales management position where I supported diverse customers purchasing software and hardware products. Through this experience, I have developed exceptional proficiency in Word, Excel, and PowerPoint.

I am extremely talented at problem-solving and thinking *on-the-spot* to provide good resolutions to complex customer inquiries. I love working with people and offer the demonstrated ability to meet deadlines in a fast-paced environment. I am particularly adept at employing empathy and understanding to diffuse difficult customer concerns.

Ms. Smith, I am certain that I will be an asset to Best Technology Company. When you meet me, you will find that I have what it takes to succeed in this challenging career. I am looking forward to taking the next steps in this process.

Sincerely,

Marie-Isabelle Arsenault
Encl. Résumé

Customer Service Representative. This letter, addressed to the recruiter, immediately grabs the reader's interest. While the candidate provides complete transparency about her disability, she expresses many strengths that the employer will value.

Cover Letter Strategist: Angelika Trinkwon

Tyler Chadwick

250.555.1234
tchadwick@careerprocanada.ca
123 Any Avenue, Salish, BC V9V 9V9

January 22, 2014

Canada Diesel Machine Co.
Salish, BC
Competition number: 12345

Re: Diesel Fitter (Mechanic) Apprentice

Please accept my résumé as application for the Diesel Fitter (Mechanic) Apprentice position. Having recently graduated in the top 10% of Maynard University's Automotive Technician Pre-Apprenticeship program, I am eager to bring my knowledge and training to an organization with such a solid reputation for excellence.

My skills include reading and interpreting mechanical drawings and an understanding of engine diagnostic equipment and mechanical tooling and measuring devices. Some of my training specific to this position includes:

- Engine diagnosis and replacement.
- Preventative maintenance.
- Automotive practices, including tools and measuring.
- Electrical diagnosis and repair.
- Brake inspection and repair.
- Suspension and alignment work.
- Oil and other fluid changes.
- Repair and replacement of tires.

I practice safe work habits, strictly adhering to safety procedures and regulations. I am able to climb ladders, enter confined spaces, and work on ships and submarines, and am willing to travel and work various shifts and overtime. In previous positions, I have been consistently recognized for my positive, productive, and proactive work ethic, which I apply to every task I undertake, and for my ability to set and achieve goals independently and collaboratively with a team. I am bondable, possess excellent communication and interpersonal skills, and am competent in a computerized environment.

I look forward to meeting with you to discuss this opportunity in more detail, specifically how my qualifications and skills can benefit Canada Diesel Machine Co. Please call me at 250.555.1234 or email me at tchadwich@careerprocanada.ca to set up an interview, or if you require more information.

Sincerely,

Tyler Chadwick

Tyler Chadwick

Diesel Mechanic Apprentice. This new graduate proves his competency by mentioning that he is in the "top 10%" of his class. The list addresses each point in the job posting with a breakdown of learned skills.

MICHAEL RUBINSKY

123 Any Avenue
Shaunavon, SK, S1S 1S1

306-555-1234
Email: michaelr@CareerProCanada.ca

Dear Hiring Manager:

RE: DZ FLATBED DRIVER

Please consider this letter of introduction as an expression of my interest in exploring employment opportunities with your organization. I have attached my résumé for your review citing a detailed overview of my skills and abilities.

I am ready and eager to take a position as a **DZ FLATBED DRIVER** and given my proven track record of having absolutely no accidents or traffic tickets since 1971, I am confident that I would be able to add value to your company.

With much to offer and an upbeat positive attitude, I feel that I can benefit a company where I hold a position and make a significant work ethic contribution to profits as a resourceful and results-driven individual.

I welcome the opportunity to discuss any of the ways that you feel my background and skills would benefit your organization. I very much look forward to hearing from you so that we can schedule an interview to talk about your expectations as my skills closely parallel those you seek to fulfill. I will devote 100% to this career position and apply excellence in time management.

Yours truly,

Michael Rubinsky

Résumé – 2 pages

DZ Flatbed Driver. The job title has been capitalized and bolded twice to ensure that the target is easily pinpointed. The address block is omitted since this applicant is hand delivering a letter to various companies during his travels across Canada.

Shelley Johnson

123 Any Avenue ▪ Calgary, AB T2T 2T2 ▪ H: 403-555-1234 ▪ C: 403-555- 4321 ▪ shelley.j@careerprocanada.ca

November 1, 2014

Teacher Hiring Department
Board of Education
123 Main Street
Calgary, AB T2T 2T2

RE: Elementary School Teacher Position

Teaching is not just my passion, it is my calling. After several years of working in the human resources industry, I am thrilled to be pursuing my true calling as a first-class educator, and am anticipating an exciting career within the Board of Education's dynamic school system. I am forwarding my résumé to you in consideration for a position as a member of your vibrant school community.

One of my strengths is cultivating a personalized connection with each student and embracing diverse learning styles within the classroom. I have excelled at forming relationships with students, placing great emphasis on building mutual respect and trust. In my current practicum, I am working with a speech pathologist to assist a young boy with speech apraxia. Although communicating with this child is very challenging, I am proud of the personal connection I have established with him and of the great strides he has made in his communications since our work together commenced.

As a Volunteer Student Teacher in China, I overcame a significant challenge of getting highly structured students to think creatively for the first time. Using wordless books, I encouraged and motivated a large class of 36 to provide individual input through creative drawing. This project resulted in great success as students cultivated their inner creativity and truly flourished! These students understood for the first time what it was like to express themselves through art.

Finally, my background in the field of human resources provides me with a range of skills that will further aid my abilities within the classroom. I am accomplished at forming and fostering relationships with diverse individuals and adapting to high-needs environments with multiple priorities and strict time constraints. In addition, I have several years of experience training, advising, information sharing, and advocating for the needs of others.

I am confident that my unique skill sets and career history can be of great benefit to your organization. I am committed to life-long learning and feel strongly about investing in a first-class school system, such as your own. Thank you for taking the time to review my application. I look forward to hearing from you soon to further discuss my qualifications.

Sincerely,

Shelley Johnson
Enclosure: Résumé

Elementary School Teacher. This letter bursts with energy as this new graduate seeks her first role as a teacher. She highlights good examples of success with students, and shows maturity and transferable skills from her human resources experience.

Matthieu Drummond

Halifax, NS | 902.555.1234 | mdrummond@careerprocanada.ca

Equipment Technologist: Industrial Engineer Ship Building Industry Sector

June 1, 2014

Beth Graham
Recruiter
ABC Shipbuilding Group
123 Address
Halifax, Nova Scotia, B1B 1B1

Re: Equipment Technologist

Dear Ms. Graham,

There's never been a more exciting time for the shipbuilding sector and I'm looking forward to starting a new career in Atlantic Canada.

Please see enclosed my résumé. As I prepare to graduate with my degree in **Industrial Engineering** from the **University of Toronto**, I am proud to bring my experience and expertise to ABC Shipbuilding Group. You will find me to be an ideal candidate for your advertised **Equipment Technologist** role.

A new entrant into the sector, my area of interest spans the full scope of Ship Building, Ship Repair, Marine Engineering, and Marine Repair. With a clean record, I already meet all of the base requirements of the Canadian Controlled Goods Program (CGP), Canadian Government Security Clearance, and U.S. International Traffic in Arms Regulations (ITAR).

Industrial Engineering Degree

Metal Fabrication Experience

Quality, Health & Safety Focus

I have already gained three years of practical work experience in manufacturing and metal fabrication. In my role, I work with heavy machinery, maintaining a perfect record of compliance with equipment installation and integration guidelines. Bringing a solid focus on Quality, Health, and Safety, I am fully committed to ensuring an optimal work environment.

As our industry sector is positioned for tremendous growth, I am eager to start as an apprentice. A forward thinking, self-motivated professional who understands that you need to "learn the ropes" before you are ready for advancement, I am keen to show you my technical abilities and other skills.

I will try to reach you next week to see if we can arrange an interview or a brief meeting. If you would like to know more before that, please give me a call or email.

Sincerely,

Matthieu Drummond

Enclosure: Résumé

Equipment Technologist. This new graduate features his degree along with transferable practical experience gained during his studies. The penultimate paragraph positions him for a progressive role in the booming sector.

Cover Letter Strategist: Marlene Slawson

Mario Beaumont
123 Any Ave., Mississauga, ON L1L 1L1
Phone: 905-555-1234   Email: mbeaumont@careerprocanada.ca

January 12, 2013

Markham Fire Department
123 Main Street
Markham, ON L1L 1L1

Re: Probationary Firefighter

Dear Hiring Manager,

I am submitting my résumé for consideration in the position of Probationary Firefighter with the Markham Fire Department. With a General Business Diploma, a Health and Fitness Management Diploma, extensive experience in the health and fitness industry, and commitment to community service, I feel that my qualifications meet the requirements for the Firefighting position.

With seven years of experience in the fitness industry, I have built a strong clientele in the community giving me exposure to people from diverse backgrounds. Passionate about helping people, I have negotiated and problem-solved fitness and health challenges, improving many lives by helping people to lose weight and become motivated to maintain healthy lifestyles. Teaching fitness one-on-one and in groups has allowed me to work exceptionally well with the public and develop superior skills in the area of public relations.

Since the age of 15, I have led a healthy lifestyle by including daily exercise and a sensible eating regimen. This has helped to improve my mental and physical strength, which I feel are strong qualifications for the Firefighter position. Finally, to prepare my application for this position, I have acquired the CPR and First Aid credentials.

I am a highly self-motivated and active person who possesses a strong interest in serving my community. I have demonstrated this commitment when I worked with a hearing-impaired teenager for over 5 years. Having worked with all types of individuals, including young children, seniors, and persons with disabilities, has enabled me to adapt to all types of situations.

As an outstanding team player, my ability to get along with my teammates on hockey teams, an arm wrestling team, and a weightlifting team is evident. Additionally, I have demonstrated commitment by organizing a power lifting competition with my group members.

Firefighting will allow me to satisfy my passion to serve others and contribute to a team environment. With an uncle who served as Captain of the Toronto Fire Department, I understand the commitment and dedication required from individuals who have selected this as a career.

Thank you for your time and consideration. Please do not hesitate to contact me for further information. I can be reached at 905-555-1234.

Sincerely,
Mario Beaumont

Enclosure

Firefighter. This letter effectively ties the individual's experience in the fitness industry with his passion for firefighting. He features strong qualifications drawn from his lifestyle and extracurricular activities.

LEON GOLD

123 Any Avenue, #100, Winnipeg, Manitoba, R1R 1R1

204-555-1234 or 204-555-1234

Email: leon123_gold@CareerProCanada.ca

July 23, 2013

John Smith, Warehouse Manager
ABC Company
123 Main Street
Winnipeg, Manitoba R1R 1R1

Dear Mr. Smith:

RE: WAREHOUSE HELP / GENERAL LABOUR / CUSTOMER SERVICE

I am presenting for your review my skills, achievements, work ethic, and straightforward approach to getting the job done well, so that we could perhaps discuss my joining your team on a full-time basis.

I can assure you that my career has paralleled transferable skills required for a general labour or warehouse position within your company. Recent experience includes wearing many hats in a manufacturing environment as an order picker, shipper and receiver, and as an assistant supervisor from time to time. Previously, I have worked receiving in-bound customer calls in the construction industry.

Warehouse / General Labour
> ➤ I am a dependable employee with a strong work ethic and solid attendance record. I have performed routine responsibilities on time by prioritizing, followed thorough, made good decisions, followed instructions meticulously, helped co-workers, and collaborate as a supportive team member and leader. Also, I understand, interpret, and convey communications with clarity.

Customer Service
> ➤ I have improved customer service and enhanced daily operations by assessing customer needs, probing questions to gather more information, and then making appropriate recommendations to help the customer benefit. I make the effort to follow up and problem-solve to find solutions quickly.

While my résumé can highlight my background and accomplishments, my potential can come out more during a face-to-face meeting. With this in mind, I look forward to the opportunity to meet with you and discuss our mutual interests and ways in which your company may gain long-term value from my skills.

Yours very truly,

Leon Gold

Résumé – 2 pages

General Labourer. This candidate successfully positions himself for a role within a manufacturing warehouse by targeting two areas in need – general labour and customer service.

MARCI FELDMAN
123 Any Avenue • Toronto, Ontario • M1M 1M1

416-555-1234

July 10, 2013

ABC Resorts

RE: HOUSEKEEPING ROOM ATTENDANT

NOC: 6455 – Ad #5555
Calgary, Alberta

My family is relocating to Alberta at the end of August and I am in pursuit of a housekeeping position. I believe that my expertise would add value and benefit your resort. For example, during the past four years I have played an active role performing systematic routine functions as a caretaker for a middle school in the Toronto District School Board. Details of this recent position are indicated on my résumé.

I realize the importance of presenting a professional housekeeping image so that guests will experience first-class service and appreciate your establishment. My contacts regularly express their gratitude in whatever job titles I've held. Past employers have recognized me for providing excellent customer service because I speak clearly while maintaining good eye contact and posture. Further, I am fluent in English and will respond politely to questions, explaining information in an easy-to-understand way.

As a self-starter who is resourceful, personable, and loyal, I am willing to undergo training to abide by your policies, safety guidelines, and hygienic practices. I find it easy to follow instructions, exercise good time management, and would be a model example for coworkers. I do not gossip and will adhere to confidentiality. Finally, I will remain calm in high-pressure situations and maintain composure to project a refined image on behalf of the resort.

I welcome the opportunity for a face-to-face interview to discuss how I can join your Housekeeping team. I may be reached at: 416-555-1234.

Yours truly,

Marci Feldman
Résumé – 2 pages

Hotel Room Attendant. This candidate effectively translates her experience as a caretaker in a school to the hospitality sector. To allay any doubts, she also expresses a strong understanding of the soft skills required in hospitality prior to closing the letter.

TARA MIDDLETON

123 Any Avenue, Vancouver, British Columbia, V1V 1V1

Tel: 613.555.1234   email: tara_m@careerprocanada.ca

April 3, 2013

Jane Smith
Human Resources Manager
City of Toronto
123 Main Street
Toronto ON M1M 1M1

Dear Ms. Smith:

Having recently completed a university certificate in Human Resources Management and Labour Relations, I am writing to enquire about entry-level Human Resources Generalist opportunities with the City of Toronto. With more than seven years of administrative and union relations experience in the social services sector, I have a breadth of practical experience and solid training that will enable me to immediately add value to your organization, and forward my current résumé for your review.

Highlights from my background that demonstrate the attributes and experience I bring to the table include:

- Active involvement in union policy development in the field of childcare and health benefits.
- Selection for intensive training in Human Rights in the workplace.
- Proven skills in crisis management and conflict resolution, which were honed through involvement in community-based crisis support for victims of violence.
- The tenacity and goal orientation needed to compete as an elite-level athlete in '06 Paralympic Games.

My work style is characterized by determination, initiative and team leadership, and I am proud of my reputation for being able to step up to any challenge and consistently delivering top quality results. My colleagues appreciate my enthusiastic approach to team collaboration, and my managers respect my can-do work ethic and grace under fire in high-pressure situations.

I am now ready to take my career to the next level, where I can channel my training and skills to support the staffing and performance management priorities of a large organization such as the City of Toronto. I would welcome the chance to meet with you in person to discuss upcoming opportunities in the Human Resources Department, and will be in contact within the week to schedule a meeting. Please feel free to reach me in the meantime at the above number and email address. Thank you for your consideration, and I look forward to speaking with you.

Sincerely,

Tara Middleton

Human Resources Assistant. This candidate who uses a wheelchair emphasizes her mobility, energy, and abilities with many action words. She does subtly allude to her disability, but keeps the letter focused on professional experience and attributes.

Cover Letter Strategist: Stephanie Clark

Anne

Brockley

123 Any Avenue
Kitchener ON N1N 1N1
Anne-b@CareerProCanada.ca
519.555.1234

July 15, 2013

Ms. J. Smith
Canada Social Services

Email Address: hr@abcsocialservices.ca

Re: Junior Agent, Job Posting 15-2008

Dear Ms. Smith:

While still in high school, I achieved the role of Assistant Manager by building on seasonal employment achievements with one employer. I am eager to once again contribute significantly to my employer's goal with a strong work ethic and "can do" spirit. My résumé in application for the advertised position of Junior Agent with Canada Social Services is enclosed.

I have gained valuable hard skills at work: supervisory, competent computer, and time and project management skills. However, perhaps some of my greatest accomplishments also stem from volunteer positions. For example, dealing with steady calls from people in crisis over a 3-hour shift at the Canadian Mental Health Centre, while providing an attentive level of service demanded stamina and critical thinking. Working with groups of up to 100 children at our Region's Children's Museum was a challenge unlike any other: keeping kids on task is no easy feat.

As my current supervisor has stated, "Anne provides service with a smile, even in stressful situations." I have been recognized for my sunny nature, hard work, problem solving, and dedication to advancing my employer's goals. I am proud of stellar reviews and positive opinions that coworkers and management alike hold of my capabilities and work ethic.

It would be my pleasure to meet your interview team and further substantiate my value as a possible future employee with Canada Social Services. Thank you for considering my application.

Yours truly,

Anne Brockley
Encl: 2 pages

Ready to Make a Difference
~ Providing Attentive Service ~

Junior Social Worker. This recent graduate's value proposition is centred on advancement in seasonal employment and volunteer work. She uses a quote from a supervisor to express her pleasant disposition.

RICHARD R. BELTZ

**MILLWRIGHT /
MECHANIC**

123 Any Avenue
Cambridge Ontario N1N 1N1
519-555-1234

July 15, 2013

Mr. John Smith, HR Manager
ABC Alberta Oil Sands
123 Main Street
Edmonton, Alberta T1T 1T1

Re: Millwright/Mechanic

Dear Mr. Smith:

Assembling machinery, analyzing how it works, and why it doesn't – these are skills that I have built from an innate ability, to the point where I am recognized amongst the top two of 22 Millwrights at my current position. Perhaps your company could benefit from my extensive experience and noted expertise. My résumé is attached for your review.

To summarize, my track record as a hard working employee is exemplified by:

→   Timely completion of assemblies, troubleshooting, repairs, and maintenance.
→   Routinely being assigned the more difficult machines and repairs.
→   Undaunted by the scope or difficulty of the project.

Furthermore, you can expect:

→   Straightforward communication style.
→   Readiness to assume responsibility and accountability.
→   Rolling up my sleeves and getting the job done right, no matter the conditions.

Thank you for the consideration. I am available for immediate relocation and welcome an opportunity to speak with you about opportunities at ABC Alberta Oil Sands.

Yours truly,

Rick Beltz
Encl: 2 pages, résumé

"I've worked with a lot of maintenance people over the years, and you are one of the best."
– current supervisor

ANALYTICAL · NO-NONSENSE · DECISIVE

Millwright. This millwright and race car enthusiast who wants to work on the Alberta Oil Fields focuses on core competencies and no-nonsense hard work to open up an opportunity for a conversation.

ESTELLE SHAPIRO
123 Any Avenue, #100, St. John's, NL, A1A 1A1, (709) 555-1234
estelle@careerprocanada.ca

July 21, 2013

John Smith, General Manager
ABC Company
123 Main Street
St. John's, NL A1A 1A1

Dear Mr. Smith:

RE: OFFICE SUPPORT WORKER

Please consider this letter of introduction as an expression of my interest in exploring employment opportunities with your organization.

My experience has helped me to develop numerous skills that can be transferred to any new endeavour. Please take a few moments to review my résumé that highlights several ways in which I may be able to help support your organization's growth both in the short-term and in the long-term.

Skills, Abilities, Work Ethic and Potential include:

- Organizational: prioritize to meet deadlines; often hand in projects ahead of time.
- Phone management: well developed customer service and listening skills.
- Fast track learning: can pick up new tasks quickly, enjoy taking on new challenges and would be willing to undergo training as necessary.

I realize the importance in today's marketplace of customer satisfaction and the delivery of top-quality service and I am willing to go the extra mile to promote these features of a successful business. Further, I will stand behind your organization with pride as an independent or team player, always abiding by rules and regulations.

Thank you for your time and consideration. I would appreciate an opportunity to meet with you in person to discuss how I help you and inevitably use my potential to contribute as a member of your team and make a positive difference.

Yours truly,

Estelle Shapiro

Résumé – 1 page attached

Office Support Worker. This candidate has extremely limited work experience; however, she has bulleted her value under the heading of "Skills, Abilities, Work Ethic, and Potential."

David Melnyk

123 Any Avenue, #100, Edmunston, NB, E1E 1E1

Mobile: 506-555-1234

david_melnyk123@CareerProCanada.ca

July 9, 2013

Edmunston Police Services
123 Main St., Bldg. 3
Edmunston, NB
E1E 1E1

Dear Recruitment Officer:

RE: POLICE OFFICER POSITION

Please consider this application for your recruitment process, as I believe I am a suitable candidate for a Police Officer position for the City of Edmunston.

It is my passion to follow my career path focused on Law Enforcement. Having worked diligently to fulfill the requirements to date, I am determined to take my career to the next level with a goal to make a positive difference and give back to the community. As an individual who maintains as well balanced lifestyle, I know how to deal with high-pressure situations. And, as a member of an ethnic minority group, we have to stand together as one to preserve the peace in a society where justice prevails.

As a highly disciplined individual, it is my intention to enforce municipal by-laws, execute warrants, prosecute criminals, and assist victims while preventing crime, fraud, and other offences. Weighing this combination of factors, I do believe that I have much to offer.

I can add value to Edmunston Police Services as a physically fit supportive team member and leader. Equally important is the fact that I always am non-judgemental, unbiased, fair, and follow instructions precisely. I do not act on impulse but rather, assess situations through analytical thinking and careful assessment.

I welcome an interview so that I can explain in more detail in a face-to-face setting how I can contribute as a leader and supportive team member. To date, I meet each qualification and have much to offer to secure a safe Canadian environment and will act as a model Police Officer for future generations.

Yours very truly,

David Melnyk

Résumé: 2 pages

Police Officer. Without much experience to share, this candidate dedicates much of the body to his understanding of the requirements of the role. He creates interest as an "ethnic minority" who knows how to deal with "high-pressure situations."

Ricardo Lee, B.Sc.

123 Any Avenue
Kitchener ON N1N 1N1

519.555.1234   rlee@CareerProCanada.ca

Candidate for: **POLICY DEVELOPMENT INTERN**

July 15, 2013

Mr. John Smith
Human Resources Manager
Ontario Public Service
123 Main Street
Waterloo, ON N1N 1N1

Re: Policy Development Intern - Environmental

Dear Mr. Smith:

Time and research show that the state of our environment impacts our health, economics, and our very future. Problems such as extinctions, water levels, water quality, and climate change benefit from government involvement. As a recent graduate of the University of Guelph's multi-disciplinary Honours Environmental Biology program, and with a strong and active interest in political processes and government policy, I feel ideally suited for the position of Policy Intern. My résumé is attached.

Although my résumé highlights related skills, education, and experience, I would like to bring your attention to the following:

 ➲ recent studies included research and presentations on topics not unlike those tackled by the Ontario Public Service. Solutions must always assess the human factor in order to be successful. My belief is that practical and reasonable solutions can and will be found for current environmental and resource problems.

 ➲ my involvement in political processes, such as with the "I Believe in Kitchener" process have given me valuable insight into the detailed steps, the building blocks required to promote change. Although necessary, change will not occur immediately nor is it likely to occur without proper background, consensus building, and buy-in from many sectors.

Our provincial government has identified the importance of protecting our natural resources and the environment; I enthusiastically endorse this decision and sincerely hope that I can join the teams currently at work in this pursuit to contribute, in some measure, to furthering this mission.

I am available at 519.555.1234, at which number you may also leave a message. It is my hope to receive a call for an interview. Thank you for taking the time to review my application.

Sincerely,

Ricardo Lee
Encl: résumé, 2 pages

"dedicated to serving Ontario, protecting the environment"

Policy Development Intern. This new graduate opens with a strong statement expressing his understanding of global environmental concerns. The first bullet relates to the organization's needs and the next features his interest in politics.

Henry Sonofsky

123 Any Avenue
Suite 100
Toronto, Ontario M1M 1M1

Tel: 416-555-1234

Dear Sir/Madam:

RE: PRESS FEEDER / MATERIAL HANDLER
...or another related position

Please consider my résumé for the position of Press Feeder/Material Handler. Past experience includes 10 years' experience in a large 24/7 printing facility mastering all facets of operating sheet-fed equipment. At this renowned printing company, I thrived in an environment where I could function as a team member or independently with minimal supervision. I knew exactly what it took to get things done properly.

At this time in my career, I am in search of new challenges with enthusiasm. I consider myself goal oriented with a strong desire to succeed and work toward outstanding results. I take pride in working hard and am able to meet deadlines and help a company save money. For example, by maintaining equipment regularly, I can help prevent downtime and loss income to a company.

Customer service is another area where I believe I could add value to your business. Over the years, I have developed confidence with existing company clients as well as establish communications with suppliers and tradespersons. Further, I see myself as having the ability to contribute as a dedicated staff person and, perhaps, as a representative of the company.

I welcome an interview session so that we can discuss my background in more detail. Please feel free to contact me at: 416-555-1234.

Thank you for your time and consideration.

Yours truly,

Henry Sonofsky

Attachment: Résumé – 1 page.

Press Feeder. This candidate is targeting some specific positions in a shrinking industry, so he keeps his opportunities open. To ensure that his résumé is not bypassed he alludes to "another related position" in the lead-in to his letter.

Cover Letter Strategist: Karen Siwak

James McDonald, B. Eng

123 Any Avenue
Oshawa, ON ✦ L1L 1L1

Cell: 905.555.1234
email: jmcdonald@careerprocanada.ca

March 1, 2014

Jane Smith
Canada Group
123 Main Street
Toronto ON M1M 1M1

Re: McKenna Group Product Development

Dear Ms. Smith:

I was greatly interested to learn that the Canada Group is recruiting EIT candidates to join their product development team, and am delighted to submit my candidacy for this opportunity. As a Mechanical Engineering graduate with a demonstrated track record in vehicle design and performance optimization, I am confident that I have the knowledge, skills and professional attributes to add immediate value to your Product R&D Branch, and forward my current résumé for your review.

I completed my Bachelor's degree with one of the top engineering schools in Canada, where I received a solid grounding on the principles of engineering design. Using state-of-the-art laboratory facilities, I had the opportunity to translate these principles into practical solutions for a wide range of design and manufacturing challenges, which enabled me to broaden and deepen my understanding of engineering best practices. Already involved in high-performance racing with watercraft at the junior level, I developed a genuine passion for auto racing while at university, and was a founding member and ultimately the captain of the university's award-winning Formula SAE team.

Upon graduation, I was privileged to be able to pursue my passion through engineering design and mechanics roles on championship-level race teams. In an environment where split-second decision-making is paramount, I was able to hone my analytical, problem-solving and team collaboration talents, and can proudly highlight that I helped the Durrell team finish among the top 5 for the 2009 season.

After three years on the professional race circuit in the USA, I have returned to Canada and am ready to pursue new career directions. I am excited about the challenges and opportunities presented in new product engineering, and would welcome the chance to discuss in person how my qualifications and experience might be of benefit to the McKenna Group. I look forward to an interview in which I can expand on the contributions I can make to your team and demonstrate the knowledge, skills and professionalism I bring to the table. Thank you for your consideration.

Sincerely,

James McDonald

Product Development Assistant. This applicant emphasizes the quality of his education and the practical skills he acquired through involvement in the race circuit. This adequately explains a 3-year volunteer engagement outside the country.

TANYA MARTIN

tmartin@careerprocanada.ca

123 Any Avenue
Calgary, AB T2T 2T2
Home: 403.555.1234
Cell: 403.555.4321

April 12, 2013

Dr. Jane Smith
Department of Psychology
University of Southern Alberta
123 Main Street
Calgary, AB T2T 2T2

Dear Dr. Smith,

In response to your need for a **Research Assistant**, please find enclosed my application. The opportunity presented is very appealing as I have a keen interest in research and psychology and am looking to apply the skills and knowledge gained from my recent degree from the University of Southern Alberta along with a deeply personal experience related to eating disorders.

I have recently completed my Bachelor of Arts in Psychology. My education strengthened my organizational and time management skills and further developed my abilities to think analytically, logically and creatively. Several course projects entailed detailed research, data collection and analysis, as well as close collaboration with others. I am also well practiced in conducting literary searches, compiling comprehensive evidence, and presenting findings in clear and concise written reports.

In my youth, I personally struggled with an eating disorder and I attended the Remedy Ranch in Florida, one of the top treatment centers in North America. I wish to deepen my understanding of anorexia nervosa in the effort to help other young people. My personal experiences have given me a solid understanding of eating disorder triggers, recovery processes, and knowledge of the various common denominators and singular factors involved.

I am available to start immediately and would welcome the opportunity to meet with you to further discuss the role requirements. I will follow up with a telephone call next week to confirm that my application was received. Thank you again for your consideration.

Sincerely,

Tanya Martin
Enclosure: Résumé

Research Assistant. This new graduate candidly outlines her personal exposure to the topic of eating disorders. Her desire to work in the role is clear; research skills gained through education and appropriate terminology is referenced throughout.

Cover Letter Strategist: Karen Siwak

ELIZABETH GILLAM

123 Any Avenue
Toronto, Ontario M1M 1M1

email: lizgillam@careerprocanada.ca
Tel: 416.555.1234
Cell: 416.555.2345

March 1, 2013

John Smith
Recruitment Manager
ABC Delta Service Group
123 Main Street
Toronto ON M1M 1M1

Dear Mr. Smith:

If the ABC Delta Service Group could benefit from the organizational and administrative skills of a versatile, solutions-oriented professional with 15 years of multifaceted experience in office management, event planning, and customer relations, then the attached résumé will be of interest to you in your search for a Special Events Coordinator.

Highlights of strengths I bring to the table include:
- ✓ Strong planning and coordination skills to ensure the seamless delivery of polished social and business events.
- ✓ The perfectionist's eye for detail that is the hallmark of a top quality administrative professional.
- ✓ Proficiency in the complete MS Office software suite, combined with the ability to swiftly and independently master new systems and software.
- ✓ Complete fluency in English, French, and Spanish.
- ✓ Extensive experience liaising with people from all backgrounds and industries.

Nine years ago, I was in the fortunate position to take a sabbatical from my full time career in order to focus on the needs of my family while my children were small. However, I made it a high priority to keep my knowledge and skills honed through active involvement in both managing a small business and also pursuing specialized training in event management. Additionally, I am called upon on a regular basis to assist community members with planning and producing their social and business events.

In my full-time career, I spent three years as a Meeting Planner and Logistics Coordinator for one of the largest IT and business training firms in North America, where I handled everything from venue selection and catering coordination to the set-up of computer equipment for training labs and the management of customer relations issues.

I am now energized for new challenges, and am excited about the chance to join a company that sets the standard of excellence for event management. I would welcome an interview in which I can demonstrate in person how my knowledge, professionalism, and drive will make me an asset to the ABC Delta Service Group, and can be reached at the above number and email address to arrange for an interview. Thank you for your consideration.

Sincerely,

Elizabeth Gillam

Special Events Coordinator This stay-at-home mother seamlessly explains her sabbatical while remaining focused on her goal of returning to event management.

Juanita Mendez

February 8, 2014

Gayle Johnson
Marketing Manager
Toronto Blue Jays
123 Bay Street, Toronto, ON M1M 1M1

Dear Ms. Johnson:

May I ask for your advice and assistance?

After completing a three-month internship with the Hamilton Bulldogs, as part of Humber College's Marketing and Advertising program, I am excited by the prospect of beginning my career in sports and entertainment marketing. I am keen to learn about your professional experience and to hear any advice you might have for someone eager to begin a career in this field.

If I could ask for 20 minutes of your time, I am sure your insights will be very valuable to me. Specifically, I am hoping to learn more about the skills and experience most required to work in the field, any challenges or opportunities this industry segment is facing, and which organizations would be a great place for a new graduate to start her career.

I have enclosed my résumé, which provides more detail about my internship with the Hamilton Bulldogs, my Marketing and Advertising studies, as well as my summer work experience, to help you learn about me.

I look forward to our discussion regarding your experience, any insights you might have on the industry, and any suggestions you may have on how to begin my career in sports and entertainment marketing. I will follow up with you by phone next week to arrange a time for such a discussion.

Sincerely,

Juanita Mendez
Enclosure: Résumé

Toronto ON · 416.555.1234 · jmendez@careerprocanada.ca

Sports Marketing Consultant. This college graduate requests an informational interview with a manager with a goal of generating an opportunity in her field of choice. A single question opens the door to a conversation with the employer.

JOE BLACK

123 ANY AVENUE, SENEVILLE, PQ, H1H 1H1
H: (514) 555-1234 ■ Email: jblack@careerprocanada.ca

January 11, 2013

TECHNICAL ENGINEER 101
DEPARTMENT OF NATIONAL DEFENCE

REFERENCE NUMBER: DND EE123

Dear recruiting manager:

I am writing to express my interest in the position of **Technical Engineer 101**, within the Department of National Defence (DND).

As can be seen in the attached résumé, I offer a unique combination of interpersonal and technical skills. My first hand experience working with drilling crews and operations, would allow me to utilize my considerable skills to the benefit of the DND.

I have been employed in the oil and gas industry for over five years. During this time, I have excelled in many different aspects of the industry including, drilling, well services, pipeline, and plant facilities. Your requirements have ignited my desire to pursue a long-term career in leveraging this experience.

For your convenience, I have listed the qualifications outlined in the job posting and highlighted my corresponding skills and experience:

Degree from a recognized university or an acceptable combination of education, training and/or experience.	**Diploma,** *(Instrumentation Engineering Technologies)*, Southern Alberta Institute of Technology, AB
Language Requirements	English Fluency and Beginner French
Experience in Health & Safety.	• **H2S Response 1**, Safety Training Center • **First Aid**, Safety Training Center • **Certified Exposure Devise Operator**, Canadian Nuclear Safety Commission

As a student participating in the Instrumentation Engineering Technologies program, I possess the knowledge and skills for the job. The focus of this program is theoretical with practical training in operation and principles of process units and their inter-relationship with instrumentation. The program also includes training in maintenance, calibration, installation, troubleshooting, and repair of pneumatic devices, control valves, electronic instruments, digital logic devices, computer based process controls, and control systems design. Knowledge in personal computer applications of instrumentation, Fieldbus, SCADA, PLC, and project management are skills earned in this program.

I learn quickly, work hard, and exercise patience. I can communicate effectively both verbally and in writing. In addition, I bring work ethic, sound judgement, drive, and potential as highlighted in my résumé.

I look forward to meeting with you, at your convenience and discussing my credentials further. Thank you for your time and consideration for this exciting opportunity.

Sincerely,

Joe Black

Technical Engineer. This recent graduate's letter focuses on five years of experience gained while attending university. He uses a "T-chart" concept to match the organization's needs with his background.

ALLAN LUCCI

123 Any Ave.
Toronto, Ontario M1M 1M1

416-555-1234
Email: allan_lucci@CareerProCanada.ca

July 9, 2013

ABC Manufacturing
123 Main St., Bldg. 3
Concord, Ontario
M1M 1M1

Via email: hr@abcco.careerprocanada.ca

Please consider me for the position of **TOOL CRIB ATTENDANT** as recently advertised in the <u>Toronto Star</u>. I believe the qualities you seek are well matched by my solid track record of current and past experience.

YOUR NEEDS	MY QUALIFICATIONS
Experienced individual to maintain, organize, and order supplies for the entire plant.	• Served in various capacities including team leadership for over 10 years. Replenished supplies by getting estimate quotations and comparison buying.
Coordinate orders with the purchasing department.	• Interacted with suppliers/vendors and check catalogue for precise and accurate decisions to be made for parts to be purchased. Selected and purchased products after testing conditions of current products.
Excellent communication, alert and highly motivated, quick to learn, and dependable work ethic.	• Displayed all the qualifications to get the job done right. These attributes would indeed complement this position. Please see the attached résumé for the pertinent details.

My résumé highlights how I could make a significant contribution as a dependable Tool Crib Attendant. I welcome the opportunity to discuss my past hands-on expertise in a personal interview.

Thank you for your time and consideration.

Yours very truly,

Allan Lucci

Tool Crib Attendant. This letter effectively uses a simple "T-chart" to list job requirements against the candidate's qualifications and experience.

Rashid Gill

Target Position: Long Haul Driver with ABC Trucking Company

July 1, 2014

Mr. Graham
Owner Operator
ABC Trucking Company
12345 12th Avenue
Langley, BC, V1V 1V1

Re: Long Haul Driver

Dear Mr. Graham,

Thank you so much for taking a moment to speak with me today. It is with great interest that I am forwarding the enclosed résumé in application for the position of Long Haul Driver.

Soon to be based in Langley BC and willing to drive across the nation, I am the ideal employee for ABC Trucking Company. I possess all the requirements for this role, including a valid class one license with a clean driver's abstract. I also have tractor-trailer experience gained through my program with Canadian Transport Trainers.

I understand that ABC Trucking Company is a progressive company that exemplifies the highest standards in the industry. You will therefore benefit from a hardworking and trustworthy professional. I know and understand the basic requirements of the Tractor Trailer Training Standards adopted by provinces across Canada. Additionally, with a clean record, I am more than willing to undergo pre-employment drug testing as well as any and all required background checks.

My schedule is flexible and I am at ease fitting in with your company's salary and benefit model, which you said is based on miles travelled.

Thank you again for the opportunity to make this submission. I am very much looking forward to speaking with you in person again.

Yours truly,

Rashid Gill

Enclosure: Résumé

Relocating to: Langley, BC | Cell: (604) 555-1234 | rgill@careerprocanada.ca

Truck Driver. This new immigrant follows up on a brief encounter with the employer. He proactively mentions all the things he has learned about the industry and the employer. He also reassures the employer by mentioning his clean record and flexibility.

MORGAN N. WATSON

123 Any Avenue • Calgary • AB • T2T 2T2

403.555.1234• morgan@careerprocanada.ca

WILDERNESS ADVENTURER
Proven Law Enforcement Leader

July 20, 2014

Jane Smith
Program Manager
ABC Wilderness Company
123 Main Street
Calgary, AB, T2T 2T2

Dear Ms. Smith:

My personal wilderness experience and passion for the outdoors combined with 25 years in the RCMP make me an excellent candidate to lead your Northern Wilderness Adventure Program. I am a dedicated professional with exceptional communication, training, and leadership skills. These competencies serve me well in my quest to become an accredited and respected wilderness guide.

For many years, I have quietly, steadily, pursued my interest in adventure tourism with activities and training that fit the role. In addition to many public service programs, such as *Cross-Cultural Education* and *Media Communications*, I have attained several wilderness-relevant certificates and completed courses in:

★ Wilderness Survival & Tracking	★ Marine Emergency Duties Level A-3 (Med A-3)
★ Mountain Challenge Outward Bound	★ Small Vessel Operator Proficiency (SVOP)
★ Powerful Leaders	★ ATV Training*
★ Maritime Operator's Certificate	★ G Division Winter Indoctrination*

** The ATV and Winter Indoctrination courses included: handling and maintenance of machines, navigation and chart work, GPS, survival skills, and chainsaw and axe handling.

While juggling the challenges of police work and mentoring a dedicated team, I continue to maintain a personal fitness regime. I enjoy cross-country skiing and snowshoeing, and take at least two kayaking excursions off the BC coast each year.

I lead by example; displaying utmost sincerity, integrity, determination, and authenticity. Those reporting to me have complimented me on my knowledge, training skills, and coaching, finding my leadership style both practical and inspiring. It would be a privilege to hone those talents and to learn many new skills through your program.

Ms. Smith, I am confident that I will make a valuable contribution as an active participant in your Northern Wilderness Adventure Program and am eager to have the opportunity to learn in such a well-respected institution. Next week, I will attempt to reach you to see whether you have had a chance to review my material and to discuss the possibility of an interview in the near future.

Sincerely,

Morgan N. Watson

Enc. Résumé

Passionate Promoter of Wilderness Adventures, Safety, and Fitness

Wilderness Guide. What an interesting opportunity for the company that hires this retired RCMP officer who has extensive expertise in the region. The letter highlights transferable competencies through the various certificates he has received.

8
Best
Cover Letter
Samples

Mid-Level
& Management

CARRIE ARONSON

123 Any Avenue
Oakville, Ontario
L1L 1L1

905-555-1234
Cell 905-555-2345
carrie@CareerProCanada.ca

FOCUS: SALES ACCOUNT MANAGER

July 20, 2013

Mr. John Smith, VP Sales
ABC Company
123 Main Street
Toronto, Ontario M1M 1M1

Dear Mr. Smith:

The hallmark of a successful sales representative is a talent for influencing people to see the merits of – and subsequently buy into – one's ideas, products, and service offerings.

I am in the market for a sales account management position. Even though my current job title may not reflect a sales-related role, I have nevertheless been able to deliver some impressive contributions to date:

- Contributed to outsourcing business success, helping to secure approximately $5 million U.S. in EBITDA – a 39% increase over prior year.
- Repeatedly capitalized on negotiations savvy, capturing as much as $20,000 in one-time savings when interacting with vendors, travel agents, and hospitality representatives from such firms as Preston Suites Hotel, Luxury Condos at One Prince West, and Aero-Express Travel.
- Personally signed on Aero-Express Travel as ABC's designated travel consultants, ultimately to offer employees additional travel savings.
- Resurrected ties with a key account that had otherwise suffered from inconsistent service in the past.

My problem-solving acumen deserves equal mention. Throughout my career, I have been tapped as the "go-to" person to resolve a wealth of issues that have identified areas of improvement, streamlined operations, and saved money.

Presently, I seek a new challenge and would like to hear about your specific sales requirements. May I call in a few days to arrange a meeting to do just that?

Yours very truly,

Carrie Aronson

Enclosure – Résumé (2 pages)

Account Manager. This candidate is transitioning from travel to sales. The bulleted portion clearly focuses on initiatives related to sales management and account management to match her target job's requirements.

EMILY ANDERSON
PO Box 1234
Salish, BC V9V 9V9
eanderson@careerprocanada.ca
250.555.1234

January 23, 2014

Geoffrey Anderson
Forward Treatment Facility
9876 Main Road
Salish, BC V8V 8V8
hr@forwardtf.ca

Dear Mr. Anderson,

It is with great enthusiasm that I submit my résumé for the position of Addictions Counsellor, which so closely matches my experience and career vision. My diverse background facilitating individual and group workshops and managing and administrating a wide variety of social and client-specific programming makes me an ideal candidate for this position.

My professional experience includes a wide range of roles related to client services, case management, and administration in vocational and rehabilitation environments, including mental health, addictions, and persons with disabilities. I have extensive experience interviewing and assessing clients for eligibility and program readiness, and making recommendations for appropriate supports and services. My case management experience includes setting realistic goals and assisting clients with the steps to achieve those goals, including facilitation of life skills, personal management strategies, and recovery and wellness. I successfully incorporate motivational interviewing techniques to foster forward movement through the stages of change continuum, and use an analytical approach to problem solving.

Dedicated to lifelong learning and knowledgeable of the twelve steps, I am continuing my education with the Mental Health and Addictions Associate certificate program at Newell College, along with disability management courses through the National Institute of Disability Management and Research (NIDMAR).

My extensive case management record demonstrates a clear competency in the challenges in managing and motivating specific groups. I have enjoyed working as a team leader, as part of a larger team, and independently in delivering the highest level of client-centered and community-based programming. My frontline experience and strategic vision have enabled me to work collaboratively with case professionals, management, and stakeholders, resulting in positive outcomes related to the issues at hand. In addition, I am a dedicated member in good standing with a variety of local and community organizations for the continued improvement of services to consumers.

I look forward to meeting with you in person to further discuss how my experience and qualifications will best suit the needs of this position. Please contact me at **250.555.1234** to set up an interview, or if you would like more information.

Sincerely,

Emily Anderson

Emily Anderson

Addictions Counsellor. This candidate leverages a background in group facilitation for a career transition. Without direct experience, she features courses, community work, and future certification in mental health and addictions.

Krista North

linkedin.com/in/infokristanorth

Midland, Ontario, Canada L1L 1L1
Phone: 705.555.1234 • Cell: 705.555.5678 • Skype: infokristanorth

Email: kristanorth@careerprocanada.ca

Excels in building relationships, internally and externally, to advance the business

January 20, 2014

Ms. Terri Smith
Human Resources Manager
XYZ Company
1234 Yonge Street
Barrie, Ontario L9Z 3P4

Dear Ms. Smith:

I am excited to apply for the position of Administrative Assistant as posted on your website. I know I have all the necessary prerequisites to meet the requirements of this office support role and heighten business operations for XYZ Company. Attached is my résumé for your review.

My solid business acumen, unparalleled customer service, and commitment to perform at the optimum have allowed me to achieve high levels of success in my sales career and will serve as the foundation in bringing value to XYZ Company in the role of Administrative Assistant.

The theme of my career has been customer satisfaction driven by my dedication, commitment, and desire to succeed. I continually took care of my client base while meeting and exceeding my employers' expectations. Working with Senior Vice Presidents of leading Canadian organizations, I have earned respect at the highest level. I regularly exceeded defined goals, achieved #1 status in sales, earned placement into the President's Club and was presented with the Brad McIntyre Award for Volunteer Service at the 2011 Community Integration Partnership annual meeting.

As a former Police Constable, I can be trusted to effectively deal with confidential business and employee information. I honed my skills in rapid note taking during my policing career and have continued to rely on my ability to translate client needs into an optimal solution.

During my absence from formal employment, I have contributed to the community by volunteering in various roles. I was involved in administering the cross-country skiing component during the 2009 Ontario Winter Games, overseeing participant registration and equipment needs. I continue to provide operational support as one of several daily volunteers with the Midland-based Community Integration Partnership, providing encouragement and guidance in life skills and community engagement to the adult clientele.

While my volunteer work is highly fulfilling and refreshing, I am energized, ready for my next career challenge, and feel XYZ Company offers the perfect fit for my skills and current career goals.

In short, I am ready to work for you; are you willing to partner with me?

Thank you for your consideration of my qualifications. I look forward to further engaging you in my interest in your organization and the value I will bring XYZ Company upon my appointment. When may we schedule an interview?

Sincerely,

Krista North

Administrative Assistant. Returning to the workforce after an extended leave, this candidate features business acumen, customer service, and commitment to perform. She includes a synopsis of community involvement and volunteer service.

❖ ❖ ❖ GAIL COMPARE ❖ ❖ ❖

123 Any Avenue, Regina, SK S1S 1S1 ❖ 306.555.1234 ❖ gcompare@CareerProCanada.ca

EXPERIENCED ADMINISTRATIVE PROFESSIONAL

July 20, 2013

Mr. John Smith
VP Client Service
ABC Company
123 Main Street
Regina, SK S1S 1S1

Re: Team Leader, Administrative Office

Dear Mr. Smith,

The description of your Team Leader job posting for the Administrative Office is well aligned with my experience and expertise. As you will read in the enclosed résumé, I am a bilingual professional with a history that encompasses client service excellence, staff training, multi-tasking in busy environments; and effective administrative, marketing, and supervisory skills.

Colleagues, managers, shift workers, and clients know they can count on me for answers, assistance, and efficient team and individual performance. I consistently demonstrate consideration for others, respect for diversity, and have exceptional written and verbal communication abilities.

My technical aptitude is outstanding. I am highly competent in a wide range of software tools and quickly grasp new programs and initiatives with ease.

I have been very successful in a diverse range of roles. These include the following:

❖ Provision of administrative management and customer service in a manufacturing plant.

❖ Organization and facilitation of exponential membership growth for a cross-Canada website.

❖ Design and production of innovative promotional material for a business machines company.

With my client service expertise, powerful organizational skills, and ability to rapidly assume new tasks and responsibilities, I am confident that I have much to offer ABC Company. In the next week, I will contact your office to ensure that my résumé arrived and to see if we can arrange a time to meet and talk about this in more detail.

Sincerely,

Gail Compare

Enc. Résumé

"(Gail) is passionate about client service, professionalism, diplomacy, and being supportive;
excellent interpersonal skills with clients, management, staff, and public."
– J. Lesson, Saskatchewan Coordinator, New Office Solutions

❖ **Action Orientation** ❖ **Solutions Focus** ❖ **Organizational Management** ❖

Administrative Team Leader. This leader makes a career change from sales to administration. From the headline through to the quote, this letter successfully mitigates all sales activities in favour of administrative responsibilities.

Stephanie Smith

123 Any Street ◆ Kitchener, ON N1N 1N1 ◆ 519.555.1234 ◆ ssmith@careerprocanada.ca

July 14, 2014

Re: Adult Day Program Assistant

Cheryl Anderson
Manager of Human Resources and Program Development
Non Profit Community Council
123 Any Street East
Waterloo, Ontario
N1N 1N1

Dear Ms. Anderson,

Please find enclosed my résumé for the above position. I believe my contract employment as an Adult Day Program Assistant with your organization has allowed me to gain knowledge and skills equivalent to those taught in the Personal Support Worker certificate program.

During my contract, I demonstrated a great deal of competence in ensuring that clients' needs were being met. I monitored and assessed client abilities, health, and attitude in a safe manner, and made certain that a friendly environment was available to all staff and clients who attended the program. Overall, I feel I made a positive contribution to the Non Profit Community Council and the Adult Day Program and I would be delighted to have the opportunity to join such a winning team once more.

In all my endeavors, I have acted successfully and with a great sense of professionalism. I am open to fulfilling a variety of functions, and am motivated to continue learning new things. Given the opportunity, I am certain I could once again be a great asset to your organization.

I am available for an interview at your earliest convenience and would appreciate an opportunity to discuss with you, in more detail, why I am an excellent match for the position.

Thank you again for your time and consideration. I look forward to hearing from you.

Sincerely,

Stephanie Smith

Adult Day Program Assistant. This candidate's previous employer is aware that she does not have the required education. Therefore, she mentions this only briefly and immediately follows with the positive qualities she brought to the contract role.

Mohammed Syed, Architect

123 Any Avenue
Ottawa, ON • K1K 1K1

Tel: 613.555.1212
email: msyed@careerprocanada.ca

March 1, 2013

Jane Smith
ABC Development
123 Main Street
Ottawa ON K1K 1K1

Dear Ms. Smith:

It takes a unique blend of design talents, business acumen, project management know-how and team leadership skills to deliver the complete design package for large residential, commercial, industrial and recreational complexes. As an Architect with more than thirteen years of experience, I have a proven track record of leveraging these strengths on multi-phase multi-million projects ranging from hospitals and hotels to multi-residential and office towers. Having recently emigrated to Canada, I am looking to join an established architectural consulting practice in the Ottawa area, and am pleased to forward my résumé as an expression of interest in opportunities with your firm.

My design style is based on the principles of classic elegance, and I am a strong believer that a building's aesthetic appeal should be evident in the broad light of day. I strive to create a harmonious balance between the building, the materials, the landscape and the streetscape, and seek to inspire without overwhelming.

From a practical point of view, I have a solid understanding of best practices in project management, and am able to implement process workflows that maximize staff productivity. In my previous capacities with Bakr Architects & Development Planners and Al Madira Architectural Consultants and Engineers, I came to be relied upon as the go-to person for complex projects that presented challenges in terms of design, hostile building environments, difficult local regulatory requirements, and high-complexity client relationship issues. Proudly, I can highlight that I consistently delivered top quality work on time and within budget.

I have extensive expertise in the complete design cycle for both direct select and competitive bid projects. With fluency in three languages, I am able to communicate and collaborate with colleagues and clients from around the world, and can navigate the inter-cultural nuances of doing business on a global scale.

As I am in the final stages of getting my Canadian accreditation, which only awaits completion of a course on the Canadian Building Code, I would welcome the chance to discuss in person how my qualifications and skills might be of benefit to your firm. I will be in touch within the next few days to see if we can arrange a time to meet. You may also reach me in the meantime at the above number and email address should you require additional information or wish to see examples from my portfolio. Thank you in for your time and consideration.

Sincerely,

Mohammed Syed

Architect. This internationally trained architect dedicates the bulk of his letter to his overseas experience and successes. He closes by reassuring the reader that he is proactively working towards achieving Canadian accreditation.

Joyce Sipowitz

123 Any Avenue, Kamloops, BC V1V 1V1 ♦ (604) 555-1234
joyce.sipowitz@CareerProCanada.ca

March 3, 2013

Ms. Jane Smith
Human Resources Department
Liquor Distribution Branch
123 Main Street
Vancouver, BC V1V 1V1

Re: Competition LDB2010:00201, Assistant Store Manager

Dear Ms. Smith,

You will find a copy of my résumé attached for your review, and for submission to the Selection Committee in application for the position of Assistant Store Manager in the 1st Street location of the Liquor Distribution Branch in Kamloops, BC

As an applicant, I am proud to put forward my 21 years of experience with the ABC Liquor Distribution Branch, as well as the following key accomplishments:

⇨ Successful completion of the LDB Assistant Manager Training Program.

⇨ Strong commitment to ensuring organizational success.

⇨ Dedication to inspiring excellence in fellow staff members.

⇨ Over 1600 hours of supervisory experience.

⇨ Leadership in process innovation and change management.

⇨ Recognition as a multiple award winning merchandiser.

I look forward to receiving your response to my application, and hope to have the opportunity to discuss my suitability for the position of Assistant Store Manager with you in the near future.

If you have any questions, or you would like to set up a time for an interview, please do not hesitate to contact me.

Sincerely,

Joyce Sipowitz

Assistant Store Manager. A long-time employee applying for a promotion in response to a job posting for an Assistant Manager communicates her loyalty, dedication, and experience in the body of the letter.

Marion Brennan — BRAND MANAGER

123 Any Ave. Toronto, ON M1M 1M1 • P: 416-555-1234 • E: mbrennan@careerprocanada.ca • www.linkedin.com/in/mbrennanici

IMAGINATION CREATION  INNOVATION

July 14, 2013

Mr. John Smith
President & CEO
ABC Advertising
123 Main Street
Toronto, ON M1M 1M1

Dear Mr. Smith:

The brand manager behind Nike's "just do it" campaign, grew company sales from $700 million to $4 billion using three words. Having worked as a brand manager to some of the world's largest companies, I understand the imagination, creation, and innovation that go into conceiving a national brand strategy.

You will see in my enclosed résumé, I am a professional brand manager with the expertise you seek. My recent accomplishments include:

IMAGINATION – Achieved 48% increase in sales after successfully reinventing a struggling brand. Elevated market penetration and bolstered market share.

CREATION – Designed the highest rated customer-relationship marketing program in its class, exceeding new membership targets by 42,000.

INNOVATION – Produced 83% sales increase and 21% product growth after developing television and point of sale campaign with celebrity endorsement.

Building a great brand affects the bottom line of every company. And, building a renowned brand relies heavily on understanding the right principles behind brand management. My innovative approaches increase sales and exceed targets.

My clients stand out because of the strategies I implement to penetrate their target markets. As a dedicated and hardworking brand manager, I am passionate about achieving results for the brands I create. Now, I would like to put my **imagination, creation,** and **innovation** to work for your team.

I will contact you on August 1st to further discuss how my qualifications meet your requirements.

Sincerely,

Marion Brennan
Enclosed: Résumé

"Marion offers stellar performance. Her client management skills are exemplary…and are held up as the gold standard for our agency. She is extremely organized, thoughtful, and proactive. She is regularly commended for an excellent job - and for exceeding expectations." VP, Creative Director, Top Advertising Agency

Increasing sales with imagination, creation, and innovation

Brand Manager. The client mitigates limited experience by discussing a well-known brand. The "imagination, creation, innovation" theme was used throughout the document to visually demonstrate brand management skills.

Cover Letter Strategist: Lynda Reeves

RENA THORNTON

BUSINESS & TEAM DEVELOPMENT PROFESSIONAL
Inspiration – Innovation – Initiative

July 20, 2013

Mr. John Smith
VP Business Development
ABC Company
123 Main Street
Toronto, Ontario M1M 1M1

Re: Business Development Manager

Dear Mr. Smith,

The experience that I offer as a successful business and team development professional more than match the requirements for your Business Development Manager. In the last decade, I grew an enterprise from $0 to six figures, was a valued team player at an international manufacturing company, and hired and trained staff to support exponential growth of a franchise.

While much of my recent success is sales focused, my earlier roles introduced me to the values of team-driven goal setting and group accomplishments. My diverse background and supporting computer proficiencies go well with my business acumen, leadership style, and award-winning sales and marketing expertise. This foundation gives me credibility in meetings with individuals at every level.

As my personal tagline shown above attests, I offer:

➡ *Inspiration:* Focused on success in every situation, I identify and implement process improvement, product enhancement, and revenue generation; and am an expert at closing deals.

➡ *Innovation:* Through in-depth discussion and probing, I uncover issues and opportunities, and produce unique solutions both within teams and in one-to-one relationships.

➡ *Initiative:* Volunteer at fundraising events for the Health Foundation. Champion product purchases and design attractive venues that contribute to outstanding donations.

Highly respected for my integrity, communication and negotiation skills, and collaborative manner, I have grown a network of clients and former associates. I know what it takes to sustain valued relationships and pride myself on being someone who rapidly generates feelings of trust and confidence.

Mr. Smith, as your Business Development Manager, I will quickly become the 'go to' person who understands what drives your business and will consistently deliver results that you are seeking. Next week, I will contact you to see if we can arrange a time to meet and discuss this in greater detail.

Sincerely,

Rena Thornton

Enc. Résumé

▪ 123 Any Avenue ▪ Mississauga, ON ▪ L1L 1L1 ▪ H: 905.555.1234 ▪ E: rthornton@CareerProCanada.ca

---

Business Development Manager. This candidate stresses business results. The opening addresses the employer's buying motivator of revenue generation and the rest of the letter supports her tagline, "Inspiration, Innovation, Initiative."

Cover Letter Strategist: Adrienne Tom

Melissa McMaster

123 Any Avenue ▪ Calgary, AB T2T 2T2 ▪ 403-555-1234 ▪ melissa.mcmaster@careerprocanada.ca

Developing Strategies ▪▪ Directing Initiatives ▪▪ Delivering Results

September 9, 2014

Ms. Jane Smith
ABC Resources
123 Main Street
Calgary, Alberta T2T 2T2

RE: **Communications Manager**

Dear Ms. Smith,

With over 10 years of experience orchestrating communication strategies, creating value-based business initiatives, and driving change management across corporate, private and not-for-profit sectors, I am well prepared to advance the communications program at ABC Resources.

As my résumé further supports, I specialize in analyzing business issues to create best-in-class communication processes and innovative brand positioning. Here are some examples of my achievements:

- Spearheaded brand-building and positioning strategies for National Network; accelerated business growth to generate over $5 million in additional revenue.

- Championed brand acquisition for Stellar Statistics; escalated revenue by 42%.

- Transformed communications program at TrueCare Society; reduced productivity challenges, improved quality of work and exceeded budget goals by 18%.

These achievements clearly outline my drive and enthusiasm for creating, propelling, and delivering high-impact communication solutions and business results.

I am eager to meet to further discuss how your open role and my matching qualifications intersect. I look forward to hearing from you soon.

Sincerely,

Melissa McMaster

Communications Manager. The cover letter is rich in words but short in length. The candidate creates high impact with stellar examples to support her value proposition and emphasize how she can benefit the organization.

MARIA S. OBA, (M.Eng.)

123 Any Avenue ▪ Vancouver BC V1V 1V1
604-555-1234 ▪ mariaoba@CareerProCanada.ca

CONSTRUCTION PROJECT MANAGEMENT
(Engineer-in-training)

July 16, 2013

Ms. Jane Smith, HR Manager
ABC Construction
123 Main Street
Vancouver BC V1V 1V1

Dear Ms. Smith:

With over 10 years' experience in delivering various construction projects, I am well prepared to contribute to the success of ABC Construction's projects. My résumé is attached in application.

I offer varied experience, including overseeing large construction projects. In particular, I would like to draw your attention to the following:

❖ I am familiar with all the documents required in project management, document control and preparing regular reports, weekly, monthly and quarterly.
❖ I have negotiated contracts, scheduled and monitored trades, prepared and updated project schedules, coordinated labour requirements, and tracked materials and equipment.

In short, I am well versed in all aspects of Project Management. However, I offer more than competent project management. Allow me to explain:

❖ I take great pride in my work and strive to improve situations, find cost savings, improve processes, save time, and otherwise make a positive business impact for my employer. My résumé contains examples of these initiatives.
❖ I approach engineering with an ethical and moral perspective. I ensure results meet standards, leave nothing un-inspected, and am committed to health and safety measures. My project page outlines past examples of engineering addressing environmental or safety standards.

My Masters in Industrial Engineering, and Bachelor in Mechanical and Production Engineering are earned in the British colony of English-speaking Nigeria. To support these credentials, I am currently in the process of obtaining the Canadian equivalency.

If my skills, experience and approach to work meet with your approval, I welcome the opportunity for an interview, in which we could explore how I might be of benefit to ABC Construction in the role of Project Manager. Please leave a message at 604-555-1234, and, should I be unavailable to take your call, I will return your call within 24 hours. In the meantime, I thank you for the consideration.

Respectfully,

Maria Oba
Att: 3 pages, résumé

MONITORS PROGRESS ➲ SUPERVISES TRADES ➲ LIAISES WITH CONSULTANTS ➲ LEADS BY EXAMPLE

Construction Project Manager. This new immigrant ensures that in addition to discussing her qualifications, she is in the process of obtaining the Canadian equivalency for her credentials as she works towards a position as an engineer.

Cover Letter Strategist: Tanya Sinclair

TANIKA CHARLES, MBA
DYNAMIC EVENT PLANNER

"It is our attitude at the beginning of a difficult task which, more than anything else, will affect its successful outcome."

- W i l l i a m   J a m e s

February 20, 2013

Jane Smith
Big Box Canada
123 Main Street
Edmonton, AB, T1T 1T1

Dear Ms. Smith:

As a visionary event planner, I offer a powerful 10-year history of masterminding innovative events and a record of groundbreaking contributions to a number of leading companies in Canada and the US. I can help Big Box Canada meet and exceed strategic goals as your **Corporate Event Manager.**

Big Box has a reputation for achieving business results with a performance and customer-driven focus. You will discover that the attached résumé illustrates my talents in these key areas. I have significant experience successfully planning events in various sizes and complexities from large-scale musical concerts to overseas executive symposiums.

My event portfolio demonstrates the experience I bring to Big Box having masterminded events for:

➡ *Musical Events: April Laping, Cindy Deon, Hendrix Sound, Jules Black*

➡ *Promotional Events: Microsoft Corporation, Estee Lauder Companies, Rogers, Shaw Cable*

You will find that these key performance indicators are only a sample of the calibre of my performance. More detail is included in the enclosed documentation. As it pertains to my leadership style, I utilize an inclusive, hands-on team approach to event planning turning vision into reality.

I believe there is an excellent fit between my leadership skills, and your need for a dynamic and engaging Corporate Event Manager. I welcome the opportunity to discuss this intriguing position in person and will follow up with a phone call to confirm the receipt of my résumé. I look forward to speaking with you in the near future to arrange a meeting at your convenience.

Regards,

Tanika Charles, MBA

Enclosure: Résumé

123 Any Avenue, Toronto, Ontario M1M 1M1 ▪ Mobile 416-555-1234 ▪ Home 416-555-2345
E-mail events@careerprocanada.ca ▪ http://www.linkedin.com/in/tanicacharlesmba

Corporate Event Manager. The document starts with a quote in the letterhead that sets the tone of the cover letter. The complete letter focuses on her "on the job" experience and comfort managing large-scale events.

Frieda Rothman

100-123 Any Avenue • North York, Ontario • M1M 1M1 • (416) 555-1234

April 23, 2013

Hiring Committee
ABC Bank of Ontario
123 Main Street
Toronto, Ontario
M1M 1M1

REF: KY001-0002 – Full-Time – Level 7 or G

It is with great interest that I apply for the position of **Learning Coach / Facilitator** as posted online.

I began my career with the ABC Bank of Ontario in 2000 and regularly earned promotions that carried increasing levels of responsibilities. I am completely familiar with the Bank's wide range of credit services, investment commodities, and deposit products with specific expertise in Small Business and Financial Consulting. In my current role as Small Business Advisor, I exceeded sales targets and improved branch profitability by encouraging client usage of Web dealing, Investor's Edge, and Telephone Banking.

You mention in your posting that the successful candidate must have:

• BCO, Mutual Funds, CSC, and PFP accreditations	**I do**
• very strong communication skills in order to effectively facilitate through various media	**I do**
• solid facilitation skills using various approaches (online, telephone, classroom)	**I do**
• familiarity with standard technology tools such as MS Office Suite	**I do**
• experience in e-learning	**I do**

Currently, I am enrolled in the Professional Coaching Program at the Raymond School of Professional Coaching where my studies concentrate on unlocking individual employee potential. The subjects I am taking stress the importance of staff teamwork, overall job satisfaction amongst employees, and better working relationships between staff, management, and clients.

It is my wish to apply these exciting theories and deliver quantifiable results for the Bank of Ontario – in the form of increased productivity, strong and sustainable performance, and enhanced service levels.

I look forward to the prospect of further conversations in a personal interview.

Yours very truly,

Frieda Rothman

Enclosure – Résumé

Corporate Trainer. This letter plays up the candidate's experience in the company and extensive knowledge of the organization, its products, and its services. The bullet points specifically address requirements outlined in the job posting.

Marsha Biderman

123 Any Avenue • Toronto, Ontario M1M 1M1
Email: marshabiderman@CareerProCanada.ca
416-555-1234

July 23, 2014

Dr. Jane Smith
Doctor's Offices
123 Main Street
Toronto, Ontario
M1M 1M1

Dear Dr. Smith:

Cosmetic care specialist in post surgery, cancer care, post-traumatic injuries, and more.

If you seek a **well-established make-up artistry professional** to complement your private practice, I offer first-hand experience in medical and non-medical skincare product lines as well as expertise in advanced cosmetic application for both men and women.

I have completed international diplomas in the study of applying specialized skincare products keeping my education current to address camouflage make-up for bruising, scarring, imperfections, and burns. At the same time, I have eased the minds of people who have completed their cancer treatments and chemotherapy sessions.

As one who has a passion and desire for training others, I teach clients how to use camouflage products. Clients, patients, and professional staff have acknowledged me for listening carefully to their concerns in consultation. I am comfortable explaining techniques in an easy-to-understand manner.

My experience spans a career in the film, theatre, photography, fine arts, and the modeling industry. In these scenarios, I provided the right make-up for the lighting involved on diverse projects.

I very much look forward to explaining in more detail how I could complement your team in a value added service or as a dedicated employee. I would welcome the opportunity to speak with you in an interview session. My résumé is included for your review. Thank you for your consideration.

Yours very truly,

Marsha Biderman
Enclosure: Résumé – 2 pages

Cosmetic Care Specialist. This candidate effectively targets a doctor's office, transitioning from a career in the media industry. To stress her goal, she opens the letter with a tagline. In the body of the letter, she addresses medical situations that may arise.

Janice Turner

janice.turner@careerprocanada.ca

123 Any Avenue
Calgary, AB T2T 2T2
Home: 403-555-1234
Cell: 403-555-4321

August 5, 2014

Mr. John Smith
Human Resources Department
ABC Flight Corp
123 Main Street
Calgary, AB T2T 2T2

RE: Airport Ambassador, Job ID #1234

Dear Mr. Smith,

If you are seeking a dynamic people person, flexible team player, and personable solution provider, I am the perfect fit for your Airport Ambassador role. Your opportunity has sparked my interest as I am searching for a new challenge applying my diverse customer service skills within a dedicated client-focused environment. ABC Flight Corp employee Sandy Miller has recommended I apply for this position and can attest to my skills.

As my résumé indicates, I have experience **connecting and engaging with a wide range of individuals** and **providing exceptional customer service** and administrative support. Many of my achievements have been attained through the successful assessment of individual's needs, the provision of consistent support, and effective oral and written communications. The following are some of my related highlights:

- Created and fostered sound business relationships with global clientele; determined customer needs for over 10 years as a Sales Representative.
- Managed a 24-hour customer support telephone line for a growing sales organization; worked diligently to provide solutions to a variety of unexpected issues or concerns.
- Collaborated closely with others as a dedicated team member; liaised between departments and senior staff to troubleshoot issues, manage logistics, and maintain a high level of customer care.

In addition to the above, I possess excellent rapport-building and networking abilities and am respected in the workplace for **managing challenges with ease.** Overall, my background includes a level of expertise that will allow me to be placed, with confidence, in your role.

Thank you for taking the time to review my application. I look forward to hearing from you soon to further discuss my qualifications.

Sincerely,

Janice Turner
Enclosure: Résumé

Customer Service Representative. This individual references the name of a current employee who can attest to her skills and abilities in the opening paragraph. Bulleted points and bolded statements draw attention to her areas of excellence.

Elise Sutton

123 Any Avenue ■ Ottawa, ON K1K 1K1 ■ 613.555.1234

October 25, 2013

Dr. John Smith
ABC Dental Practice
123 Main St.
Ottawa, ON K1K 1K1

Dear Dr. Smith:

After three years in the United States, I have returned home to Ottawa. The city has seen explosive growth in the last five years, and I see great opportunities in helping you grow your dental practice.

I have extensive experience as a Dental Receptionist/Treatment Coordinator. As you are well aware, Ottawa has seen several practices establish themselves in the last few years. Patients have a choice, and service above the norm will keep them coming. To provide first-class patient care, a practice must work as a team, be well organized, and have excellent communication. To that end, my strengths include:

♦ Knowledgeable in dental procedures, which facilitates patient communication—able to educate them on the treatments required, and answer any of their concerns.
♦ Ability to schedule patients for maximum productivity.
♦ Experienced in helping a new practice become established.
♦ Leadership skills, organizational skills, and the capability to excel in a stressful environment.

Given my background, I am confident I can contribute to the continued growth of your practice. My enclosed résumé will provide you with details of my experience.

I will call you in a couple of days to see if we can schedule an interview, and explore this mutual opportunity.

Sincerely,

Elise Sutton

Enclosed: Résumé

Dental Receptionist. This letter leads in with a solid explanation that succinctly addresses a gap in employment. It follows this up by outlining the candidate's strengths in bullet form.

ABDUL BILAL ALI

123 Any Avenue
Hamilton ON L1L 1L1

905.555.1234
aba@careerprocanada.ca

▪ Applying exceptional technological skills to optimize organizational performance ▪

January 31st, 2014

Ms. Martin
Hi-Tech Inc.
123 Any Street
Kitchener, ON N1N 1N1

Re: Desktop Support Analyst

Dear Ms. Martin,

With more than four years of experience and a reputation for outstanding technological and problem solving skills, I have great interest in your search for a Desktop Support Analyst. I sincerely hope to show you that I may be your ideal candidate.

My education includes four years of **Computer Engineering**, two years each at two universities in two countries. Life and politics interrupted my studies before I finally arrived at my destination as a landed immigrant in Canada, via Sudan, Egypt, and Russia (along the way I added English and Russian to my native Arabic).

In Canada, I achieved my **Network and Internet Security Specialist** Diploma. My education continues with many self-study simulations and training; in fact, I landed my current position without any training in VOIP. I was hired based on my promise that I would learn the AVAYA system within three days, which I did. This year, I plan on adding the required A$^+$ certifications to my credentials.

Optimal performance of all integrated systems is my goal. Currently, I support 500 staff working for a leading provider of outsource call centre solutions as its only Network Administrator in the Head Office location.

With thorough planning, my meticulously executed duties result in **no loss in productivity due to down-time**. In addition, please note that I have implemented many IT projects, ranging from $40K - $200K. My work has been recognized with a Certificate of Appreciation conferred by the company's President.

My technical abilities are detailed on the attached résumé. Confident that my skills meet your needs, I hope to hear from you with an invitation to an interview. In the meantime, I extend sincere thanks for your time.

Abdul

Mr. Abdul Bilal Ali
Encl: résumé

Desktop Support Analyst. This new immigrant effectively mitigates his basic English language skills with a solid letter. He successfully shifts focus by emphasizing international experience, education, and credentials.

EMILIO COSTAS

123 Any Avenue, Edmonton, AB T1T 1T1   ecostas@careerprocanada.ca   (780) 555-1234

ABC SafeSavers   May 30, 2013
123 Main Street
Edmonton, AB   T1T 1T1

Attention: Mr. John Smith, Employee Services
Re: **Employment opportunities in ER (Emergency Response)**

Dear Mr. Smith:

The events of the last few years have reaffirmed the fact that the world will likely never be the safe place that it ought to be. We have seen corporate, government, and public security become increasingly threatened by the emergence of emboldened terrorist groups operating far abroad from their traditional home bases. We have seen software and equipment malfunctions continue to cause disasters, despite recent advances in technology. And we know that we will continually be challenged in our ability to predict, prepare for, and respond to natural disasters such as earthquakes and fires.

I specialize in helping organizations to prepare for and mitigate the consequences of any such unforeseen emergencies - to be ready to respond, and to demonstrate to the marketplace that they are a safe bet for doing business. As the Emergency Planning Manager for a mid-sized Edmonton-based airline (NorthAl Airways), I single-handedly created and currently operate the company's entire ER function. The ER opportunity with ABC SafeSavers is just the type of work that I excel in, and if brought on board, I can envision bringing immediate improvements in safety to your organization. Here are a few things I would bring to SafeSavers:

➢ **Proven leadership in Emergency Response**… The comprehensive program that I developed and operate for NorthAl Airways is a model of excellence, and it includes an ER Centre, ER Plan, ER Training Program, and a Bomb Threat Training Program.

➢ **Outstanding communication skills**… A skilled writer, I have written (both solely and as part of a team) several large documents for my airline employers, including an 800-page ER Manual, a Flight Attendant Manual, and several ER and Flight Attendant training programs. An experienced presenter and trainer, I have trained thousands of airline employees and have more recently given speeches to numerous groups on ER preparedness.

➢ **First-hand understanding of how businesses run**… I spent several years as the owner/manager of a busy ice cream shop and, more recently, was one of a small group of individuals that started NorthAl Airways from scratch.

➢ **The character and the drive to make things happen**… Many different challenges (both as an employee and as a volunteer) have made me able to work well with others, especially with difficult personalities in stressful circumstances. I perform well both on solo assignments and when coordinating activities with others. My highly organized, detail-oriented, quality-focused approach has consistently brought positive results.

Thank you for reading my résumé. I would really like to share with you my ideas about how I could build a top-notch ER function that protects ABC SafeSavers well into the new millennium. Let's book an in-person meeting for sometime in the next two weeks. I will set some time aside on my calendar for this purpose. In the meantime, if I may answer any questions you might have, I'm only a phone call away.

Sincerely,

Emilio Costas
Enclosure (résumé)

Emergency Response Manager. The letter effectively outlines real-life security issues that concern employers today. The bulleted section delineates pertinent examples of the candidate's specific emergency response qualifications.

Cover Letter Strategist: Tanya Sinclair

J.T.

123 Any Avenue
Montréal, QC H1H 1H1
H: (780) 555-1234
C: (780) 555-2345
jt@careerprocanada.ca

"Jason is a true leader in every sense of the word. He brings to his work integrity, focus, and clear directives. He leads by example. His clients benefit from his patience, knowledge and understanding. Jason is warm, inviting and a true Networking Guru."

— Mike Martin,
Employment Coordinator,
ABC CSC

JASON C. TURNER

Bilingual Career Development Specialist

February 26, 2014

Jane Smith, Recruitment Manager
ABC Consulting
123 Main Street
Montréal, QC H1H 1H1

RE: Employment Resource Coordinator Posting, Reference # ERC123

Dear Ms. Smith,

Employers often say, *"It's hard to find good help."* Fortunately, with the attached résumé I endeavour to simplify, and perhaps complete, your search for an Employment Resource Coordinator by showcasing my skills as a resourceful, goal-oriented, and compassionate professional dedicated to the provision of quality career services.

Your mission at ABC Consulting is to *"Identify strategies that move you from success to significance."* My qualifications and skills as a bilingual career development specialist are highlighted below and are an excellent fit for your goals and this position.

- ⇨ 10⁺ years career development experience in both public and private sectors.
- ⇨ Articulate facilitator with a finesse for public speaking in both French and English.
- ⇨ Empowering team player and leader with a caring, comprehensive approach to services.

I am confident that my ability to develop strong relationships and positively influence others will greatly benefit ABC Consulting as it has my previous employers.

After you have reviewed my résumé, I would welcome an opportunity to discuss this exciting opportunity further and talk to you about the value that I can bring to the organization. Let's talk soon!

I will contact your office within the week to confirm receipt of my résumé and to schedule an appointment at your convenience. Thank you for your time and consideration.

Warm regards,

Jason Turner

Enclosure: Résumé

Jason C. Turner*...Delivering Quality Services to Clients with Integrity & Dedication!*

Employment Resource Coordinator. This career practitioner makes every effort to impress. He features his bilingualism, distinguishes himself as "good help," and clearly shows that he has researched his target company.

Carol Hill, B.Sc., M. Eng - Engineering Manager

BETTER TECHNOLOGY ⅄ BETTER RESULTS

July 7, 2014

Daniel Sterling

Chief Engineer

XYZ Organization

123 Any Street

Victoria, BC V1V 1V1

Re: Engineering Manager

Dear Mr. Sterling,

It can be challenging to design a plan that stimulates creativity and encourages peak performance from engineers. My strengths lie in doing this while decreasing costs and improving productivity. Working for world leading companies like Cisco and IBM, I have implemented best practices in my area of expertise and am confident of the value I have to offer your company. The enclosed résumé supports my application for the position of Engineering Manager.

I am confident that my advanced education combined with award-winning performance makes me an ideal candidate for this position. My leadership success is built on my ability to plan, organize, and evaluate projects while coordinating staff to achieve company objectives.

Below represents a sample of my recent accomplishments:

⅄ Decreased operational expenses $120K, reduced equipment and labour fees to outsource "re-work."

⅄ Eliminated redundancies and improved efficiency 32%; combined design and engineer teams to fill knowledge gap.

⅄ Exceeded savings targets $8.5K in the first year and $18.9K in the second year on product development testing.

⅄ Secured $155K contract to research Radio Frequency Identification (RFID).

My credentials include a combined Masters in Engineering and Business Administration along with a national award in marketing and a performance award from one of the world's largest networking companies. Raised in a successful business-oriented family, I am keenly aware how my role as an engineer contributes to a company's bottom line and the importance of streamlining operations and improving efficiency.

XYZ Organization is clearly a market leader with a reputation for the pursuit of excellence in the IT & Engineering industry. I believe there is a strong match between your requirements for this role and my engineering management experience. If you agree, I would be pleased to discuss, in detail, my candidacy for the role of Engineering Manager. In the meantime, thank you for reviewing this information, I appreciate your consideration.

Best Regards,

Carol Hill, B.Sc., M. Eng, M.B.A. - Engineering Manager

Enclosed: Résumé

BETTER TECHNOLOGY ⅄ BETTER RESULTS

Oshawa, ON L1L 1L1 | (905) 555.1234 | carolhill@careerprocanada.ca | http://www.linkedin.com/in/carolhillxx

Engineering Manager. This candidate has worked in leading companies so she lists her previous employers' names prominently in the first paragraph. Her academic credentials are evident in the header, body, and signature line of this letter.

Rabinder Singh, BA

Toronto ON M1M 1M1 · rsingh@careerprocanada.ca · (416) 555.1234

August 9, 2014

Michelle Porter
Human Resources Manager
United Way Toronto
120 Adelaide Street East, Suite 123
Toronto, ON M1M 1M1

Dear Ms. Porter:

The United Way's long history of building a better Toronto is a cause that I believe in wholeheartedly. Seeking to unite my enthusiasm for the United Way's community development initiatives and my six-year career in administration, I am submitting my enclosed résumé for any future office administrative positions.

Throughout my career, I have provided support to senior personnel, maintaining administrative and financial controls, coordinating workflow, and preparing reports and presentation materials for international audiences. In my former position as a Senior Administrative Assistant, I was frequently called upon to train new staff, improve office procedures, and coordinate large administrative projects to ensure that strict deadlines were met.

As you will see in my résumé, my key contributions include:

· Collaborated with department director, producing annual budget figures and associated reports.

· Developed procedure manual for training new hires, achieving improved productivity among junior staff.

· Executed detailed and summary financial reports for departmental analysis and comparison.

· Created office templates in MS Word, streamlining internal requests and file management systems.

I would be pleased to arrange an interview to discuss how my experience, knowledge, and enthusiasm will be of benefit to the United Way of Toronto. I will follow-up with you Monday next week to discuss the future administrative needs of the organization.

Sincerely,

Rabinder Singh
Enclosure: Résumé

Executive Assistant. This cold call letter effectively opens the door to a shift from the private sector to not-for-profit. The letter's opening successfully positions the candidate to perform administrative work within the community development sphere.

Cover Letter Strategist: Marian Bernard

DENISE DOTREEV

123 Any Avenue
Aurora, Ontario
L1L 1L1

905-555-1234
Mobile 905-555-2345
d-dotreev@CareerProCanada.ca

Targeting management roles in:
FINANCIAL ANALYSIS · DATA ANALYSIS

July 21, 2013

Mr. John Smith
I.T. Manager
ABC Telecommunications
123 Main Street
Toronto, ON M1M 1M1

Dear Mr. Smith:

If there was ever a theme to my career, it could be described as my wanting to locate the most efficient route possible within the shortest amount of time – without sacrifice to overall quality.

Case in Point: While at Top Telecommunications, I participated on a 4-person I.T. team challenge with supporting a weekly subscriber base of 5 million customers spanning all of the U.S. and Puerto Rico. Because of the sheer volumes of work that we faced, we uncovered new data sources as well as innovative processes and procedures that led to the drastic reduction of weekly report production times from 5 days to 1 day – a drop of 80%.

In addition, new codes were being set up in response to different cable TV packages offering a variety of network bundles. My team and I determined a way to interpret the data that improved overall staff productivity because this initiative reduced coding times and heightened accuracy levels.

A resourceful problem-solver, I diligently tackle what is in front of me. I persevere until the job is done because I resolve to take on tough challenges and aspire to succeed – even in the face of challenging goals. With a solid track record behind me, I am confident that I can do the same for you.

I would be pleased to have the opportunity to set up an in-person meeting so that we may discuss your needs and how I might be able to meet them. I will follow up with you in a few days; in the meantime, you are welcome to contact me if you seek any additional information.

Thank you for your time, consideration, and attention. I look forward to hearing from you.

Yours very truly,

Denise Dotreev

Enclosure – Résumé (2 pages)

Financial Analysis Manager. One major achievement is emphasized as a "Case in Point." This example expands on areas such as teamwork and process improvement to highlight management qualities.

Jose Alvarez

123 Any St. Montreal QC H1H 1H1
514-555-1234 | ja@careerprocanada.ca

Certified Financial Risk Manager (FRM)
Leading from a position of technical strength, customer focus and outstanding results.

January 31st, 2014

Ms. Able, Human Resource Manager
ABC Finance Inc.
123 Yonge Street
Toronto ON M1M 1M1

Re: Finance Specialist

Dear Ms. Able,

As a Financial Risk Manager with industry leader Money Inc., I hold the key competencies and have met the challenges inherent in the position of Finance Specialist.

Working in an intense and invigorating environment with a global leader of risk management consulting and hedge outsourcing, my team and I have devised state-of-the-art solutions. Heavily involved in research and development, my role has been pivotal to industry-leading solutions such as a reinsurance framework that runs extremely large-scale valuation and pricing runs with unprecedented speed and accuracy.

> ‣ Subject matter expert in risk management information and technology
>
> ‣ Record of groundbreaking solutions that generate revenue
>
> ‣ Astute relationship management with colleagues and clients alike

My providing service at a high standard led directly to an international company signing a full outsourcing agreement, transforming a previously non-guaranteed income of approximately $1.5 Million to a guaranteed contract that has grown from $2 Million to $5 Million.

I invite you to review my résumé for details of my performance and technical expertise, as well as examples of my communication and people skills. I am as comfortable programming code as I am in the boardroom, delivering sales presentations, securing client confidence and ensuring business growth.

Eager to return to Ontario (I recently married a Torontonian), I am looking for a new opportunity where I can continue to drive positive improvements, growth and financial results. I welcome your invitation to an interview, and look forward to speaking with you.

Yours truly,

Jose Alvarez

Financial Risk Manager. This candidate effectively features many strengths through a thoughtful letter design. He focuses on business and results throughout the body, and adds personality by closing with a note explaining his reason for relocation.

MARK A. BROWN

123 ANY AVENUE ☐ OTTAWA, ON ☐ K1K 1K1 ☐ H: 613-555-1234 ☐ mabrown@careerprocanada.ca

DEDICATED TRANSPORT PROFESSIONAL
Supply Chain I Freight Distribution I Logistics

June 1, 2013

Mr. John Smith
VP Supply Chain
ABC Logistics Company
123 Main Street
Ottawa, Ontario K1K 1K1

Dear Mr. Smith:

ABC Logistics Company has a reputation for delivering solutions to address the challenges faced by your customers. I exceed client expectations with a service-oriented approach that gains additional business and drives operational performance. I now seek new challenges in an organization where service is a priority. The position of **FREIGHT DISTRIBUTION MANAGER** would certainly seem to offer an opportunity to leverage my expertise and enhance customer satisfaction at your company.

My reputation for motivating personnel and elevating productivity as a Dock Foreman comes from a hands-on approach. With a background in fleet coordination, freight distribution, and logistical forecasting, I enhance transport operations. I am confident that my abilities would be an asset to ABC Logistics Company. The following demonstrates my success in these areas:

- Contributed to company growth by increasing sales through a *Factory Gate Pricing* initiative which established competitive rates and improved operational productivity.

- Streamlined the transportation function using innovative logistical methods and achieved significant reductions in rates for Ontario and Quebec while realizing over $10.4 million in annual savings.

This is a synopsis of only two accomplishments – imagine what I could do for your company. The details of my other achievements are available in the enclosed résumé.

I bring additional value with a wealth of excellent contacts in third party logistics. My strong negotiating skills and ability to promote collaboration have served me well in rendering effective agreements for all stakeholders while building solid supply chain performance. Also, I possess a keen sense for business development with a solid understanding of technology which will impact future business opportunities at ABC Logistics Company.

ABC Logistics Company is recognized as an industry leader in going beyond the call of duty to service your clients. It would be a pleasure to discuss the position of Freight Distribution Manager as this opportunity offers a perfect marriage between your organization and my dedication to the highest standards of service.

Sincerely,

Mark A. Brown

EXPERIENCE + DETERMINATION + INITIATIVE = ROI

Freight Distribution Manager. Although this professional has spent most of his career as a Dock Foreman, he uses a headline to target various roles in the transportation industry. He adds value with two strong bulleted accomplishments.

Cover Letter Strategist: Lynda Reeves

VANESSA PERCIVAL, BSc

H: 403.555.1234 | C: 403-555-6789 | E: vpercival@careerprocanada.ca

HUMAN RESOURCES & CLIENT SERVICE PROVIDER

July 6, 2014 *Sent via email and hardcopy*

Walter Powell
President
ABC Company
123 Any Avenue
Calgary, Alberta T0T 0T0

Re: Human Resources Generalist

Dear Mr. Powell,

For several years, I have held diverse roles with accountabilities similar to those described in your posting for a Human Resources Generalist. Prior to moving to Alberta last month, I was HR Coordinator at a clinic in Brazil. Always eager to grow, I am developing my Canadian expertise and credentials through a formal Human Resources Management Program.

Always proactive, I constantly seek new challenges and have been recognized in all my positions for getting up to speed in far less time than the norm. My style is very collaborative, and I love to share information with others and offer suggestions to make tasks more efficient. I provided formal training and scheduling as leader of a team of four, and have provided informal mentoring in most of my other roles as well.

Wherever I have worked, I earned a reputation for:

⋄ Being well-informed – becoming the person others would turn to for help and support.

⋄ Knowing how to deal with personnel issues that arose – managing them all promptly and tactfully.

⋄ Taking an active role in employee retention – providing orientation and training programs.

In addition to those talents, I managed site operations at the clinic when the director was absent. I recruited and trained staff, organized clinic flow, managed budgeting, and ensured timely head office reporting. My roles were always multi-faceted. For instance, as a client counsellor for another clinic, I took on marketing and sales strategies – boosting one product's sales by 15 times in only one month.

It would be an honour to join your team as your Human Resources Generalist. In a few days, I will contact your office to ensure that my résumé arrived. Perhaps at that time, we can talk about it in more detail.

Sincerely,

Vanessa Percival

Human Resources Generalist. This internationally experienced candidate mitigates the targeted employer's potential concern up front. She states that she is developing her Canadian expertise and credentials through a formally recognized program.

LATOYA B. JOHNSON, CHRP, MHRM

• 123 Any Avenue Apt 123 • Toronto ON M1M 1M1 •
H (416) 555-1234 • latoya@careerprocanada.ca • C (416) 555-2345

STRATEGIC HUMAN RESOURCES GENERALIST
"Providing people solutions with bottom-line results!"

February 26, 2013

Jane Smith, Recruitment Manager
ABC Manufacturing
123 Main Street
Toronto ON M1M 1M1

RE: **Human Resources Posting, Reference # HR123**

Dear Ms. Smith,

If ABC Manufacturing is seeking a dynamic, results-oriented human resources professional with strong communication and leadership skills, then I believe we have good reason to meet!

Your organization has a reputation for operational excellence as shown by your recent ranking as one of the "50 Best Employers in Canada." I would like to exceed expectations by using my talents to support your exceptional work. I feel this position is an excellent career opportunity and match for my skills and experience.

Highlights of my background include:

- *Progressive leader with over five years' experience as a Human Resources Professional.*

- *Hands-on expertise in all functional areas of strategic human resources planning working in both unionized and non-unionized environments.*

- *Exceptional project management skills and the ability to lead and influence others while communicating effectively towards the achievement of company goals.*

My experience is complimented by a strong education that includes the national Certified Human Resources Professional designation, which keeps me up to date with Canadian employment legislation and emerging industry trends. As the attached résumé indicates, I am also a life-long learner who is committed to excellence and believes in actively giving back to the community through volunteer work.

I am eager to discuss this intriguing career opportunity with you further. I will contact your office within the week to confirm receipt of my résumé and to schedule an appointment at your convenience. Thank you for your time and consideration.

Warm Regards,

Latoya Johnson, CHRP, MHRM

Enclosure: Résumé

Human Resources Professional. This individual clearly has done her homework by investigating ABC Manufacturing. She has chosen to flatter them by featuring their ranking as one of the "50 Best Employers in Canada."

Cover Letter Strategist: Linda Schnabel

BETH DRUMMOND

123 Any Ave. Calgary, AB T1T 1T1 • 403-555-1234 • beth.drummond@careerprocanada.ca

ACCOMPLISHED HUMAN RESOURCES GENERALIST

"Building HR infrastructure and culture that aligns with organizational strategy..."

August 4, 2013

Mr. John Smith
President & General Manager
ABC Solutions
Calgary, AB T1T 1T1

Dear Mr. Smith:

If ABC Solutions could benefit from a talented professional who has demonstrated an ability to create, from-the-ground-up, an efficiently functioning HR department, I invite you to read on. It would seem that my skills and background match perfectly your current search for a professional with strategic vision and creative capacity.

In 2006, I was hand-picked by the CEO of Vintage Corporation to establish its first human resources department. Vintage is a private company that has established itself as the leader in asset performance management software solutions for capital intensive industries such as mining, steel, pulp and paper, oil and gas, and utilities.

In short, I was being asked to create formal processes and policies for all aspects of human resources including training and development; recruitment, selection, and on-boarding; terminations; compensation, salary, and benefits; health and safety; talent management and employee retention. No small feat, but one that I tackled with enthusiasm and successfully achieved.

Some additional "home runs" in overseeing this special mandate include:

• **Established** HR as a trusted partner with management, staff, the Board, and external stakeholders;

• **Led** a smooth facility move which allowed for seamless and uninterrupted business activity;

• **Received** Employee of the Year Award in 2007 for outstanding contribution to the organization.

A unique feature of my profile is this: I have married an understanding of financial, bottom-line focus (profit orientation) with a talent for serving as an employee advocate and senior management advisor (people and relationship orientation). Therefore, although human resources is not always seen as a profit centre, my approach is one that takes into account the impact any initiative will have on the organization's financial health and strategic goals. This combination of skills has given me a distinct advantage and helped to create my credibility with the executive team and the Board.

On a personal note, I take an active leadership role as a board member for ALPA (Association of Little People of Alberta), which has given me a special opportunity to help educate the public on achondroplasia dwarfism, a common genetic disorder that has been highly misunderstood. However, thanks to the work of organizations like ALPA and recent televised programs such as "Little People, Big World," the message is rapidly spreading to show that individuals with achondroplasia, and other forms of dwarfism, have the same potential for success as average-sized adults.

If ABC Solutions would find merit in the tangible benefit I can bring to an HR department (particularly if it means growing one from the ground-up), as well as my work as a well-networked community member, I would like to describe in greater detail the ways I can support your organizational goals as a new and growing company.

In the meantime, thank you for your consideration of my credentials, which you will find in the attached résumé.

Sincerely,

Beth Drummond

Human Resources Manager. This candidate focuses on her powerful background from the headline through the opening and body of the letter. She alludes to her physical disability only in passing by honing in on the leadership role she played in ALPA.

MARCO ENCHILLA

Angus, Ontario L1L 1L1 | marcoenchilla@careerprocanada.ca
C: 416.555.1234 | H: 905.555.4321

October 2, 2014

Ms. Brenda Picard
Human Resources Officer
ABC District School Board
1234 Main Street West
Simcoe, Ontario
L9Z 1P1

Dear Ms. Picard:

Mr. John Smith, HVAC/Energy Supervisor, has referred me to you as he feels I would make an excellent addition to your team. Attached is my résumé for the **Heating, Ventilation, Air Conditioning and Controls Technician (HVAC)** appointment posted on your website.

John and I worked together for four years at both HVA Specialty Inc. and YYZ Services / ABC Company and he can attest to the high calibre of work I provided to each employer and my customers.

My career has afforded me extensive experience and opportunity to repair new and older model heating, ventilation, air conditioning and refrigeration equipment. I am certain this breadth of knowledge would be of benefit in servicing the diversity of equipment and systems utilized within your School Board facilities.

In addition to my **TSSA G1 Gas Technician Certificate** and my **Refrigeration and Air Conditioning Systems Mechanic Certificate (313A)**, I have pursued additional industry training including:
- Environmental and Natatorium Indoor Air Quality and Dehumidification Systems.
- Ozone Depletion Prevention.
- Cryogenic Cascade Freezers and C02 Incubators.
- Implementation of Quality Improvement Process for HVAC Trades.

I am reputed within the industry for attentively and expertly maintaining a wide range of HVAC equipment including: building automation controls, air handling units, variable speed drives, boiler heat recovery equipment and feed water systems, motor control equipment, general electrical distribution systems, centrifugal and reciprocating chillers. In summary, my depth of experience encompasses all facets of the job description.

I have worked in educational institutions, servicing the HVAC needs of Georgian University and Acme College and am excited at the opportunity to join the ABC District School Board.

Thank you for your time and consideration of my candidacy. After granting me an interview, I am certain you will understand why John Smith feels I would be the ideal candidate as your HVAC Technician.

I anxiously await your call.

Sincerely,

Marco Enchilla

HVAC Technician. This letter references the name of a contact that has recommended the candidate for employment. The first two paragraphs draw the reader in and compel the employer to read on.

Cover Letter Strategist: Maureen McCann

Elizabeth Norris, P. Eng
INDUSTRIAL TECHNOLOGY ADVISOR
123 Any Ave. Calgary, AB T1T 1T1 ♦ 403-555-1234
e.norris@careerprocanada.ca ♦ http://www.linkedin.com/in/enorristechadvisor

May 13, 2013

Mr. John Smith
Assistant Deputy Minister
ABC Government Department
123 Main Street
Calgary, AB T1T 1T1

Ref: Industrial technology advisor specialized in mechanical engineering

Dear Mr. Smith,

This letter is in response to your search for an industrial technology advisor specializing in mechanical engineering.

My interest in the government department stems from my passion working at the forefront of product development. A professional engineer with a keen interest for research and development (R&D), I can offer my experience in small to medium sized enterprise (SME) management, product design, marketing, product commercialization, and technical sales. My attraction to the industrial technology advisor position is based on the vital role the government department plays in connecting people and resources to improve the promotion of scientific and industrial research throughout Canada.

As an engineering industry project manager with more than ten years of experience, I understand the importance of timing technological advances with the market especially when working with SME's. I have a proven ability to develop, design, build, and test new technological innovations. This, coupled with my strength in project management has improved the productivity and profitability of the companies for whom I have worked.

I specialize in helping organizations prepare for and deliver engineering services by providing:

♦ **Proven leadership in design cycle:** From theory to proven models, I have successfully engineered concepts that work to deliver technological advances for small and medium sized enterprises.

♦ **Expertise working with SME's:** My professional experience has allowed me to *push the edge* of technology. As operations manager of XYZ Company, I developed, designed, built, and tested an innovative and environmentally friendly product for the oil and gas service industry.

From these achievements, you can see that my comprehensive understanding of the correlation between new technology to market, cash flow, and return on investment (ROI) is based on first-hand experience.

Although my present position has been stimulating and rewarding, at this point in my career I am confidentially exploring new and interesting challenges where my broad expertise can be fully utilized.

I welcome a personal meeting so that we can discuss your requirements and my background in much greater detail.

Sincerely,

Elizabeth Norris, P.Eng
Enclosed: Résumé

At the Forefront of Product Development

Industrial Technology Advisor. This letter employs a "keyword" strategy. It incorporates key phrases such as "product design" and "project management" throughout the document and includes acronyms and abbreviations as appropriate.

Rose Dollinger

123 Any Avenue ⊙ Abbottsford, BC V1V 1V1
Phone: (604) 555-1234 ⊙ Email: rdollinger@CareerProCanada.ca

June 10, 2013

Mr. John Smith
Public Service Agency
123 Main Street
Abbottsford, BC, V1V 1V1

Re: Competition #23456, Web Learning Project Coordinator

Dear Mr. Smith,

I have attached a copy of my résumé for your review, and for submission to the Selection Committee for the above noted competition with Public Service Agency.

The timing of this exciting posting coincides perfectly with my search for an opportunity to apply my creative web site design and development expertise in a dynamic team environment with a diverse range of clients.

After reflecting on the passion that has driven my career as a Professional Web Designer, Instructor, and Business Owner, I believe that the following attributes closely match the requirements for this position:

- ⊙ More than five years of experience as Principal Web Designer and Owner of Live Wire Web Design.

- ⊙ Over three years of experience as a Web Technologies Instructor working with adult learners.

- ⊙ Above average project management and relationship building skills.

- ⊙ Outstanding creative problem solving abilities.

- ⊙ An exceptional ability to meet the challenges of making the web useful, usable and universally accessible.

I appreciate your consideration and I look forward to having the opportunity to further discuss my suitability for the position of Web Learning Project Coordinator with you in the coming weeks.

Sincerely,

Rose Dollinger

Internet Project Coordinator. Transitioning to a permanent government position, this professional leverages her current role as a self-employed business owner by focusing attention on her expertise in the bullet points.

MIKE KETTLE

123 Any Street
Keswick, ON   L1L 1L1

Phone: 705.555.1234
mikekettle@careerprocanada.ca

February 10, 2014

Human Resources Department
Financial Credit Union Limited
Unit 1- 123 Any Street
Barrie, ON   L1L 1L1

Dear Human Resource Manager,

Please accept this letter and the accompanying résumé as my application for the Senior Investment Advisor/Wealth Management Manager position posted January 30, 2014 on workopolis.com.

In the capacity of Senior Financial Services Representative, I have successfully assisted clients with understanding and purchasing investment and financial planning products over the past five years. A great deal of my experience has included educating clients about Financial Institution's investment products and managing high value accounts.

I feel I would be a great asset to Financial Credit Union as we share common values in aggressive sales growth, while ensuring that our clients' needs are being met at all times.

I am highly organized and am proficient with computer applications. Additionally, as my professional endorsements and experience will highlight, I have a commitment to quality service. I also demonstrate the ability to effectively cope with challenging situations while meeting company objectives.

I would welcome the opportunity for an interview to further discuss my suitability for this role. Please also note that I am willing to travel for an interview and relocate for this position if I am the successful candidate. I can be reached at 705-555-1234.

Thank you for your time and consideration. I look forward to hearing from you.

Sincerely,

Mike Kettle

TOP PERFORMING FINANCIAL PLANNER / INVESTMENT SPECIALIST

Investment Advisor. This letter features industry experience and strengths that coincide with the company's requirements. To ensure that the candidate is not disqualified, he mentions that he will travel and relocate if necessary.

123 Any Avenue Calgary, AB T2T 2T2	**NATHAN JONES, P.Eng** ■ ■ ■	403.555.1234 nathan@careerprocanada.ca

September 9, 2014

Mr. John Smith
ABC Office
123 Main Street
Calgary, Alberta T2E 2T2

RE: Manufacturing Engineering Manager

Dear Mr. Smith,

As a seasoned senior-level professional, I bring more than 15 years of experience in manufacturing engineering, specifically in the establishment and evolution of technical test engineering processes and practices, along with the leadership of diverse teams.

As my résumé further describes, I have a compelling combination of management expertise and the abilities to conceive, develop, and execute strategies and initiatives for sustainable manufacturing and test processes. I currently manage a team of eight engineers and oversee all activity on several multi-million dollar projects. Each project under my guidance has successfully transferred high-revenue products to market through volume manufacturing facilities around the world.

My leadership style can be classified as firm and decisive, yet respectful and rewarding; I thrive at fostering relationships and engaging with a diversity of individuals and stakeholder groups. The relationships I have forged with industry designers and external suppliers successfully led to increased test process performances and reduced development time on over 80% of my projects last year.

I am seeking a new challenge that will tie together my core management principles with an organization in need of a leader that can enhance the development of high quality products to generate larger profits. I believe my experiences would easily transfer to the position you are seeking to fill, and I would welcome the opportunity to sit down and further discuss how your needs and my qualifications intersect.

Sincerely,

Nathan Jones, P.Eng
Enclosure: Résumé

Manufacturing Engineering Manager. This candidate features team and project leadership. He emphasizes how his related skills have resulted in success, using appropriate industry language throughout the letter.

Luca Davinci

123 Any Ave ▪ Suite 100 ▪ Toronto ▪ Ontario ▪ M1M 1M1 ▪ Canada
☎ 416-555-1234 (home) ▪ 416-555-2345 (mobile)   ⌨ lucadavinci@careerprocanada.ca

January 29, 2013

Ms. Jane Smith
Hiring Manager
B2B Company
222 Main Street
Toronto, Ontario M1M 1M1
Canada

Dear Ms. Smith:

When I discovered the position of **On-line Direct Marketing Manager** on the *B2B* website, I wasted no time in applying. This position appears to be a perfect match for my skill set. I am a confident, sharp individual with experience in successful market strategy conceptualization and implementation. Please accept my enclosed résumé and this letter as my application for the position of **On-line Direct Marketing Manager.**

My attached résumé outlines my academic and work history. As a result of these experiences, I can offer you the following qualifications:

- Ten years of direct On-Line Marketing experience
- Proven leadership, problem-solving, and decision-making skills
- Experience in tracking and analyzing consumer and client behaviour
- In-depth understanding of, and experience with, *B2B* and its service offerings
- The ability to create highly cost effective e-CRM marketing systems
- Solid technical expertise in the areas of computer/Internet development software and design.

Given my experience and drive, I would quickly use my creative and intuitive approach to directly enrich my team while contributing to *B2B's* profit. Throughout my career, I have demonstrated an uncompromising attitude and a work ethic that stands alone, and I go far beyond the "9 to 5" work mentality.

I look forward to meeting with you soon, to further discuss how I can contribute to the ongoing success of *B2B.*

Sincerely,

Luca Davinci

Enclosure: Résumé

Marketing Manager. The bold job title quickly directs the reader to the position for which this individual is applying. The bullet points list applicable supporting qualifications.

DR. SABRINA ALI

123 Any Avenue, Oakville, Ontario, L1L 1L1, CANADA (905) 555-1234
dr.ali@careerprocanada.ca / www.dr.ali.careerprocanada.ca

January 15, 2013

IMG-Ontario
123 Main Street, Suite 100
Toronto, ON M1M 1M1, CANADA

Attention: Mr. John Smith, Program Director

Please accept this letter as a formal application to the *International Medical Graduates Program* in Ontario, within the Family Medicine Stream. I have enclosed my Curriculum Vitae for your consideration.

I am a dedicated Primary Health Care Physician from Cairo, Egypt with more than 15 years of experience in both private and clinical practice. Delivering essential accessible heath care to vulnerable populations, especially the elderly and terminally ill, is a personal priority. I am committed to providing a balanced approach to preventative medical care that includes promoting wellness and the timely diagnosis and treatment of illness. Overly extensive workups stress both the patient and health resources. By taking good medical histories, I am able to diagnose potential health issues and to order only those diagnostic procedures that are necessary.

As you will read in my Curriculum Vitae, my skills are well suited to delivering medical services in underserved areas and I welcome the opportunity to do so in Ontario. I believe my personal attributes of honesty, skill, compassion, and ethics would enhance my performance in the role of a medical practitioner in Ontario. To date, I have been recognized with several nominations, honours, certificates, and scholarships, and I intend to practice with the same degree of integrity in Ontario.

I received my LMCC in June 2012 and am ready and willing to relocate anywhere in Ontario. As a Canadian citizen and Ontario resident, I have had the opportunity to become familiar with the many community resources that are available in Ontario. I am committed to the Canadian Code of Ethics, and I strongly identify with the Health Promotion Strategies concept.

I trust that you will find all of the documents presented with this application complete and in good order, so that I may continue to move smoothly through this process. I look forward to working as a Family Physician, and I am ready to serve the people of Ontario.

Sincerely,

Sabrina Ali, MD

Enclosure: Curriculum Vitae

Medical Practitioner. The opening paragraph offers a clear explanation of the reason for the letter. In this concise document, Dr. Ali provides ample information about her background and directs the reader to her curriculum vitae for further details.

Samantha Knight BScN

123 Any Avenue
Ottawa, ON K1K 1K1

(613) 555-1234
(613) 555-2345
sam@careerprocanada.ca

May 26, 2013

Jane Smith
Human Resources Director
Grace Hospital
123 Main St.
Ottawa, Ontario K1K 1K1

Dear Ms. Smith:

An unselfish desire to care for others is an important quality for anyone entering the health and medical field. This genuine desire led me to pursue a Bachelor of Science Degree in Nursing. Having recently graduated, I am now armed with the knowledge and skills required to excel at my chosen profession.

While earning my degree, I built a solid background of transferable skills to the health and medical field. The enclosed résumé will give you a brief overview of those skills. Here are some of the highlights:

Nursing: ER and Mayo Clinic Special Care Unit experience taught me to handle stressful situations with poise and professionalism. Interacted directly with patients and their family, which enhanced my nursing skills. Received academic honours and scholarship. What this means to you is that I can take my share of the patient load, and relieve your overworked nursing staff.

Human Relations: Relevant experience developed leadership skills and expanded my commitment to helping others. Many patients have complimented me on my great bedside manners; when patients are well taken care of, they will not be as demanding, and stress is reduced for all nurses. What you get is a contributing team player, able to provide excellent patient care while holding her own.

Given the opportunity, I am confident that I can become a valuable part of your team. I have exceptional academic credentials, solid experience, and a profound devotion for helping people in need. Nursing is not just a job; it's a big part of who I am.

I am available to start immediately, and would like to schedule an interview with you at your earliest convenience. I look forward to hearing from you soon.

Sincerely,

Samantha Knight

Enclosure: Résumé

Nurse. Two strongly bolded qualifying areas demonstrate that this candidate will be a productive team member from the start. The letter ends with a reminder that she is available to start right away.

GRANT MATHESON

123 Any Avenue, Prince George, BC V1V 1V1
Home: (604) 555-1234 Cell: (604) 555-2345
Grant_Matheson@CareerProCanada.ca

April 14, 2013

Mr. John Smith
Human Resources Advisor
ABC Pulp Mill
123 Main Street
Enderby, BC V1V 1V1

Dear Mr. Smith

I have attached a copy of my résumé for your review, and for submission to the Selection Committee for the posted position of **Operations Supervisor** with ABC Pulp Mill in Enderby.

My interest in forwarding my application to you for this position is due in part to my desire to work for a pulp mill that has undergone the type of in-depth modernization that ABC underwent in 2011, as I was a key player in a similar operation.

Upon review of my credentials, you will find that I bring the following key competencies to contribute to your team:

- More than 33 years of experience in Pulp Operations, with 14 years supervising multi-disciplinary teams.
- A proven talent for leadership and team building.
- Accomplishments in productivity and equipment performance improvements.
- Established reliability and safety performance records.
- A proactive approach to applying predictive and preventative maintenance.

Thank you for your consideration. I look forward to hearing from you in the near future.

Sincerely,

Grant Matheson

Operations Supervisor. This letter effectively minimizes a large career gap due to an illness by bulleting the candidate's top qualifications, according to the selection criteria.

Phyllis Paton

123 Any Avenue ❖ Edmonton, AB T1T 1T1
780.555.1234 ❖ ppaton@careerprocanada.ca

❖ Benefits & Payroll Professional ❖

July 20, 2013

Ms. Jane Smith
Human Resources Manager
ABC Company
123 Main Street
Edmonton, Alberta T2T 2T2

Re: Payroll and Benefits Administrator

Dear Ms. Smith,

With knowledge and expertise as both a payroll and benefits administrator, I have what ABC Company needs to provide outstanding service, support, and customer management. Exceptional problem identification skills, varied software expertise, and a passion to improve processes and communications make me the ideal candidate for your advertised position of Payroll and Benefits Administrator.

Highly regarded for my business focus and interpersonal strengths, I demonstrate tact in negotiation and collaboration. I am dedicated to helping others understand complex terminology and leading them smoothly through the steps. I build solid relationships with internal and external contacts, and end-users; ensuring that procedures and policies are easy to understand and follow.

Armed with strong analytical skills, I frequently uncover opportunities and deliver solutions that meet the unique needs of diverse organizations and its clientele. Some examples of where I took initiative include:

❖ Researched carriers and producers, and presented a solution for a move to a Everyone Life Group plan affecting 1000 employees.

❖ Analysed reports and invoices; revealing and resolving charges for staff no longer with the company and others whose information had not been processed correctly.

❖ Performed cost-benefit analysis and procured folders and material for a staff orientation program, adding value with the new more professional presentation.

In the enclosed résumé, you will learn more about my qualifications and wide range of experience. That will help to reinforce the value that I offer as your Payroll and Benefits Administrator, but only upon meeting you will I be able to adequately describe how well suited I am for that position. Later next week, I will contact you to discuss options for us to talk in more detail about all that I can do for ABC Company.

Sincerely,

Phyllis Paton
Enc. Résumé

Detail Oriented ❖ Process Driven ❖ Solutions Focused

Payroll and Benefits Administrator. This matter-of-fact candidate uses a letterhead as a pointer to the job title and expertise that this qualified applicant brings. The bullet points in the letter list achievements that are transferable to the target position.

Steven Tremblay
123 Any Street
Grange, BC V9V 9V9
250.555.1234
stremblay@careerprocanada.ca

ENVIRONMENT | INNOVATION | SAFETY

January 2, 2013

Carla Crawford
Nexcor Oil Canada
P.O. Box 123
Postal Station A
Calgary, Alberta T9T 9T9

Dear Ms. Crawford,

A productive, solution-focused and internally motivated **Power Engineer** with exceptional troubleshooting and problem-solving abilities, I am seeking a challenging opportunity where I can contribute my environmental knowledge and expertise to the growth and development of a proactive organization.

My strengths include working collaboratively with multi-disciplinary teams to improve production, maintain smooth operations, and reduce costs. I am mechanically inclined and able to diagnose, repair, and improve operations of systems and equipment.

As a Safety Representative, I contributed to the development of safety policies and procedures, performed area safety audits, and developed lockout and confined space procedures. I have an exceptional ability to interpret and disseminate complex plans, policies, and procedures, and bring enthusiasm and adaptability to my work, along with a proven ability to motivate and train individuals and teams, demonstrating effective leadership through example. Some key highlights of collaborative accomplishments include:

- Annual savings of $300k/yr over a three-year span by reducing effluent system defoamer costs.
- Installing and commissioning a heat recovery system, resulting in 8% steam load reduction.
- Developing process graphics, operational procedures, and employee training.
- Installing and commissioning automated demineraliser system, resulting in chemical savings.
- Designing, installing, and commissioning Saalasti presses, resulting in increased boiler efficiency.

I value lifelong learning and have completed several health, safety and job-specific courses and seminars, earning various licences and certifications.

I believe that my qualifications and experience can contribute to Nexcor Oil Canada's vision and goals for growth. I look forward to discussing how my background and skills would best meet the needs of your organization and enhance the role of the Power Engineer. Please contact me at **250.555.1234** to set up an interview, or if you require any further information.

Sincerely,

Steven Tremblay
Steven Tremblay

Power Engineer. This candidate features broad qualifications and adds impact with a list of neatly formatted achievements. Rather than targeting a specific job posting, he addresses the company's need for an engineer with environmental savvy.

Martin Yao

123-456 Any Avenue
London, ON, N1N 1N1, Canada

Phone: 519 555-1234
E-mail: myao@careerprocanada.ca

March 15, 2013

Ms. Jane Smith
Hiring Manager
ABC Executive Enterprise
123 Main Street, Suite 321
Burlington, ON, L1L 1L1, Canada

Dear Ms. Smith:

Please accept this cover letter and the attached résumé as my application for the **Management Process Consultant** position with *ABC Executive Enterprise*, as posted in the *Lite Business School* Career Centre.

I am interested in this position because my passion lies in the consumer goods industry. The posted position matches my skill areas in the following three ways:

- As an experienced Project Manager, I consistently met clients' expectations and finished projects before their deadlines, while simultaneously handling several projects in different cities.
- As an Account Manager and Senior Sales Director, I learned to be outstanding at establishing and maintaining client relationships and delivering presentations.
- As a co-founder of two successful start-up businesses, I tactically honed my strategic planning and self-motivating abilities.

I strongly believe that my proven leadership, communication skills, and management experience, along with my desire to contribute as an executive and a project manager, will bring value to your organization. I have performed the analytic and marketing functions in over 1000 marketing research projects, priming me to meet – and often beat – deadlines under great pressure, and I welcome the challenges of the **Management Process Consultant** position at *ABC Executive Enterprise*.

I am looking forward to meeting you so that we can discuss my suitability in further detail.

Thank you for your consideration.

Sincerely yours,

Martin Yao
Enclosure: Résumé

Process Consultant. The candidate carefully selected his points in this letter to match the posted requirements. The individual focuses his bullets on listing his previous positions that fit each requirement.

PATRICK T. SMITH

PSMITH@CAREERPROCANADA.CA
NIAGARA FALLS, ON L1L 1L1 | 905.555.1234

May 31, 2014

Mr. Byrne Roget
National Search Firm
123 Any Street
Halifax, NS B1B 1B1

Dear Mr. Roget:

Please accept my application for the position of **Production Manager** with your manufacturing client as advertised on your website.

As a Production Manager in the food processing industry, I offer more than 20 years' experience ensuring that quality standards are met and customers' expectations are consistently exceeded in a fully integrated processing facility.

Senior management often commends me for my collaborative, hands-on, management style, where I exceed performance expectations while managing costs, improving efficiency and meeting strict quality standards. My mechanical aptitude allows me to significantly reduce operational costs even further by maintaining plant equipment myself.

During the peak production cycle, I had 40 employees reporting to me and I was responsible for ensuring that production levels were staffed appropriately. I trained my team to become more productive and efficient while ensuring product quality 100 percent of the time.

In addition to my production management skills, I have experience operating and maintaining a high-pressure boiler and ammonia refrigeration plant, am self-reliant and pay strict attention to the regulatory requirements of my industry. I have also developed strong professional relationships with suppliers, customers and regulators, ensuring revenue growth for my employer.

As someone who is self-directed and who pursues excellence in production quality, I would be pleased to meet with you and your client to discuss the organization's needs in detail.

Please contact me at your convenience to arrange a time to meet. You may reach me at 905.555.1234.

Sincerely,

Patrick T. Smith

Production Manager. This career changer effectively targets appropriate positions through a national search firm. His strategy includes stating the target position several times in the letter.

Marc Graham – PROJECT COORDINATOR

North Bay, ON P1P 1P1 ▪ (705) 555.1234 ▪ marcg@careerprocanada.ca

PROJECT MANAGEMENT ▪ GOVERNMENT COMMUNICATIONS

July 16, 2014

Elizabeth Sparks
Service Canada
123 Any Place
North Bay ON P1P 1P1

Re: Project Coordinator

Dear Ms. Sparks,

My professional reputation is built on my ability to advance the mandate of the Government of Canada. With more than 10 years of experience delivering creative solutions within the public sector, I have implemented operational plans, managed events, and developed a comprehensive network within the government.

Service Canada has an excellent reputation for giving Canadians fast and easy access to programs and services. Having successfully authored and edited communications products on behalf of the Government of Canada, I value an organization where communications, strategy, and project management drive performance. It seems clear to me that my expertise supports the requirements you have outlined for the position of Project Coordinator. I therefore submit my résumé demonstrating my qualifications for this role and the value that I offer.

My career with the federal government spans ten years, working to establish best practices, analyze policies, and deliver project plans. Confident in conflict management, my depth of experience navigating the political landscape enables me to resolve situations quickly and efficiently.

Building collaborative networks, developing strategic communications, and performing in-depth research and analysis are but three of the competencies I have to offer Service Canada. I take great pride in my ability to create enduring strategies, synthesize information, and coordinate responses on behalf of the Government of Canada.

I welcome the opportunity to meet with you to learn more about this exciting position and describe my government and management experience in greater detail. Please feel free to contact me directly by phone at (705) 555.1234 or by email at markg@careerprocanada.ca

I look forward to collaborating with Service Canada and using my communications, strategy, and project management expertise to achieve the department's mandate.

Sincerely,

Marc Graham
PRI # 111222333
Enclosed: Résumé

...supporting quality and excellence for Canada

Project Manager. Targeting a position within Service Canada, this public sector candidate relies on 10 years of experience in the federal government. The complete letter is positioned on his work within the Government of Canada.

	123 Any Avenue
	Kitchener ON N1N 1N1
	519-555-1234
	andrec@CareerProCanada.ca

July 15, 2013

Mr. J. Smith
Human Resources Manager
Canada Property Management
123 Main Street
Kitchener, ON N1N 1N1

Re: Property Manager

Dear Mr. Smith:

The key to creating a strong team is to set a common goal—a valuable lesson learned early in my career while with the Canadian Football League (CFL). As realtor, leasing agent, and drive team member, I keep my employer's goals in mind and make them mine. Canada Property Management's goal of "property management with integrity" is in sync with my own values, and with an eye to advancing my career in property management, I submit my résumé in application for the advertised position of Property Manager.

The most important attributes of a highly effective property manager are:

- Communication skills needed to liaise between tenants, trades and management
- Logistical coordination and time management skills to juggle the many facets of the job
- The ability to foresee and plan in order to avoid as many emergencies as possible
- The capacity to react calmly and rationally in emergency situations

I come by these skills and attributes naturally, and through the various positions that I have held.

I thrive on hard work and enjoy taming chaos. I challenge myself to "find a way and make it work." I also believe in the long-term benefits of collaborative communications, which again is a way of finding a way to make it work. A "win-win" solution benefits everyone, builds relationships, and safeguards reputations. I look for such solutions whenever possible. However, when needed, I communicate firmly and with resolution. Overall, I am someone you can depend on, a strong employee who will champion your company.

Thank you for taking the time to consider my résumé; it is my goal to contribute to your team and further the goals of Canada Property Management, and I hope to hear from you soon with an invitation to an interview.

Yours truly,

André Clark
Att: 2 pages

Property Manager. This candidate's opening hits hard. He leverages his experience in the CFL as an opportunity to connect with "like-minded" decision makers who want to take a chance on him for a property manager role.

Cover Letter Strategist: Stephanie Clark

BARBARA CLARK

123 Any Avenue SW
Calgary AB T3T 3T3

Bachelor of Nursing ✦ Diploma of Nursing

403.555.1234
bc@careerprocanada.ca

Relocating to British Columbia Imminently

January 31st, 2014

Ms. Fenstrom
Human Resources
Good Health Centre
123 Any Street
Vancouver BC V1V 1V1

Re: Psychiatric Nursing

Dear Ms. Fenstrom,

Nursing is a calling, and psychiatric nursing, dealing with dual issues of mental health and addictions, requires a specialized skill set. I feel fortunate that I discovered this to be my ideal niche while on an eight-week placement during my nursing training. With a special interest in working cross-culturally (I trained in New Zealand on Asian and Maori cultural perspectives), I am confident that the needs of the Good Health Centre's Aboriginal Unit will be well met with the experience, skills, and education I offer.

It is not my "style" to speak highly of my skills and attributes as I prefer to simply do the job I love to the very best of my abilities. Highly interested in the position with Aboriginal Mental Health, I shall have to balance my hesitation with a need to convince you of my qualifications!

My background is comprehensive: similar work in New Zealand and most recently, in Calgary; work in clinical, hospital, in-home and on-site situations; individual and group therapies and counselling; and extensive work in creating and delivering training and presentations in psycho-education. I have deep knowledge of mental health and addiction issues, treatment, support, and crisis management. I've applied this knowledge to support clients and their families, and also to mentor and coach new staff. I've worked with every age group.

I have developed my knowledge with ongoing professional training, most recently in School Shooter Threat Assessment, Critical Incident Stress Management and Preceptor Training refresher. A complete list is available on my résumé. I've shared my knowledge with many presentations to alcohol and drug workers, primary and secondary health care providers, and community groups.

Of course, the day-to-day also involves maintaining files and accessing additional resources from partnering service providers. I enjoy the variety of tasks and skills needed, but overwhelmingly, what keeps me working in the psychiatric health care arena is the immense gratitude when small gains are made, and the feeling of having a positive influence on a family's or person's well-being.

If your ideal candidate is focused and decisive, organized and reliable, experienced and expert, I hope that you will consider my application. I extend my thanks for your time and consideration.

Sincerely,

Barbara Clark
Encl: résumé

Psychiatric Nurse. A unique letterhead features this candidate's credentials and intelligently expresses her need to relocate. She proves further value by demonstrating relevant experience and a true passion for the field.

Valerie Black
123 Any Street
Hamilton, ON L1L 1L1
vblack@careerprocanada.ca
905-555-1234

July 6, 2014

ABC Company
123 Any Road
Burlington, ON L1L 1L1

Attention: John Grove

Dear Mr. Grove,

Please consider my résumé for the position of Expeditor, as posted on the Canadian Job Bank website. My extensive background has provided me with many job skills that include negotiating contracts, teamwork, attention to detail and working under pressure.

Some key points that are relevant to this opportunity include:

- Reviewing and monitoring inventory levels for several departments.
- Applying solid experience using MS Word and Excel spreadsheets.
- Working closely with the Accounting Department to verify prices and delivery of goods.
- Comprehensive problem solving, communications and decision making skills.

Working for my previous employer for 14 years, I had the pleasure of dealing with several of your internal customer service associates and the local sales representative for the London area. Their integrity, professionalism and dedication to providing best possible solutions is a value that I share and I would welcome the opportunity to become a part of your team.

If you are looking for a highly motivated person who is committed to the highest standards of work performance, I would welcome the opportunity to meet with you for an in-depth discussion. I am available for an interview at your earliest convenience, please contact me via phone at 905-555-1234 to arrange a time and date for us to meet.

Thank you for your time and consideration. I look forward to speaking with you soon.

Best regards,

Valerie Black

Purchasing Expeditor. This candidate takes advantage of experience working with employees of the targeted company. She clearly mentions dealing with several internal customer service associates and the regional sales representative.

Cover Letter Strategist: Tanya Sinclair

JENNIFER A. MCCALLA

◗123 Any Avenue ◗ Toronto ON M1M 1M1 ◗ H. (416) 555-1234 ◗ jen1@careerprocanada.ca ◗ C. (416) 555-2345

INNOVATIVE QUALITY CONTROL SPECIALIST

January 15th, 2013

Jane Smith, Recruitment Manager
ABC Manufacturing Canada
123 Main Street
Toronto ON M1M 1M1

RE: Quality Control Supervisor Posting, Reference # QCM123

Dear Ms. Smith,

In response to your posting for a Quality Control Supervisor, I am enclosing my résumé for your review. Given my proven record of work performance and experience in quality control and manufacturing, I am confident that I would be an excellent candidate for this position and an ideal fit for ABC Manufacturing Canada.

I pride myself on being an innovative, results-oriented, hands-on individual with progressive management experience. My management style strongly emphasizes teamwork and relationship building founded upon clear communication and expectations. An evaluation of my résumé will further acquaint you with my background and qualifications for this position.

Your Requirements:

- ◗ Five years of progressive supervisory experience.
- ◗ Quality control training and/or certification.
- ◗ Solid hands-on understanding of the requirements of ISO certifications, along with excellent communication, computer, and leadership skills.

My Qualifications:

- ◗ 10+ years of progressive manufacturing experience and growth.
- ◗ Certified ISO 9001 Auditor through York University.
- ◗ Demonstrated leadership capability in driving operations excellence and exceeding corporate goals. Strong facilitator with solid computer proficiency.

In review of my résumé, you will note my career growth and experience. What it cannot illustrate, however, is the degree of professionalism, resourcefulness, and dedication that I offer as an employee. A personal conversation will enable us to discuss how I can contribute to the success of your company. As requested, my salary requirements for this role range from $55k to $65k and are negotiable. I look forward to exploring this opportunity with you in the near future.

Regards,

Jennifer McCalla

Enclosure: Résumé

Quality Control Specialist. Excellent use of bulleted lists of "requirements" and "qualifications." This format demonstrates how the individual exceeded the job posting's requirements – bypassing the fact that she has not actually held a supervisory title.

MARJORIE LOW – SOCIAL SERVICES PROFESSIONAL

123, Any Avenue · Winnipeg, MN · R1R 1R1 · H: 204.555.1212 · mlow@careerprocanada.ca

September 1, 2013

Mr. John Smith
Social Services Research Unit Manager
ABC Social Services
123 Main Street
Winnipeg, ON R1R 1R1

Dear Mr. Smith:

It was a pleasant surprise to read about the opening for the position of **Research Associate** with ABC Social Services in the Winnipeg Free Press. It is with a keen interest that I am submitting the enclosed résumé outlining how this position matches the qualifications I have to offer.

You will find that my work experience is rooted in my passion for bringing people together with a common objective of serving the organization and the communities that they live in. As a counsellor, I use an attentive heart to extrapolate information and bring various points of view together. By drafting scripts in a clear and concise communication style, I am able to assimilate data and deliver results. Here are some examples of my achievements:

- Nurtured relationships, to coordinate a Project Steering Committee and Advisory Group consisting of 35 professionals from Canada, Mexico, and Australia.
- Persisted in exceeding objectives despite working with people with very busy schedules and unpredictable work situations.
- Conducted the background research that led to the ultimate funding and successful publication of documentation on critical programs to support youth affected by crime and their families.
- Developed a *Community Residential Facilities* manual that initiated discussion about best practices. This brought focus on community integration and brought institutions out of isolation.

My specialty is in correctional reintegration methods; however, I am also well versed in the needs of various demographics. I work from an eclectic perspective with an experiential approach as a counsellor. I use a variety of research methods that place an emphasis on transparency. Relying on my finely tuned intuition, I follow leads to obtain relevant information in knowledge transfer. Using my research, I draft succinct clear copy for proposals that have rendered award-winning documents.

ABC Social Services seems to be progressive in your approach, an indication of your organizations' willingness to "think outside the box." This is a perfect match with my dedication to bringing creative solutions forward. It would be my pleasure to meet with you to discuss the position of **Research Associate**. I appreciate your time and consideration.

Sincerely,

MARJORIE LOW

| Empathy | Creativity and Innovation | Rationale |

Research Associate. Motivated to move from the corrections to the research side of social services, this candidate leverages her limited experience at the front lines. She emphasizes background research, team coordination, and document writing.

KATHARINE PATTERSON

123 Any Avenue, Vancouver, BC V1V 1V1   katpat@careerprocanada.ca   (604) 555-1234

ABC Retailing   May 30, 2013
123 Main Street
Vancouver, BC   V1V 1V1

Attention: Mr. John Smith, General Manager
Re: **Retail store management opportunity - Vancouver**

Dear Mr. Smith:

The challenges of large retail store management are numerous, ongoing, and complex. They demand an experienced, proven leader who is motivated, organized, focused, and skilled at managing both the valuable assets and the many processes that typify a large operation. As one such leader, I would like to meet with you to discuss opportunities with the ABC Retailing team.

I bring to you:

➢ Fourteen years of experience with a major grocery chain - culminating in my current senior management position – during which I became recognized and awarded for bringing outstanding results.

➢ A record of consistently achieving a broad spectrum of financial and non-financial objectives through long-term visionary, medium-term strategic, and short-term tactical activities.

➢ A total commitment to recognizing the value and the efforts of my staff, promoting a harmonious workplace, and ensuring top-notch customer satisfaction.

I would love to discuss the opportunity to manage a mid to large-sized retail operation for your company. I am certain that my long record of successes in this field would be a tremendous asset to your organization.

Thank you for receiving this letter and résumé. I will contact you in one week to discuss the status of my application. In the meantime, please don't hesitate to get in touch with me if I may provide any further information. I look forward to talking with you soon.

Sincerely,

Katharine Patterson
Enclosure (résumé)

Retail Store Manager. This manager has only worked for one employer. She capitalizes on her progressive experience and awards in her first bullet point. By further addressing the employer's buying motivators, she de-emphasizes a lack of education.

ADELE HANSON

123 Any Avenue
Mississauga, Ontario
L1L 1L1

905-555-1234
Cell Phone 905-555-2345
Email: a-hanson@CareerProCanada.ca

July 21, 2013

Mr. John Smith
HR Director
ABC Company
123 Main Street
Toronto, Ontario M1M 1M1

Dear Mr. Smith:

POSITIONS OF INTEREST: SALES MANAGER / NATIONAL SALES MANAGER

When I accepted a sales position with DEF Company in 2000, I was challenged with rebuilding relationships with clients who had suffered from inconsistent service and support in the past. In record time, I was able to gain their confidence, and I take pride in knowing that these clients are still loyal – 7 years later.

Listed below is a sampling of contributions that I have been able to deliver to date:

- Led 3-person sales force who have since doubled revenues from $3 million to $6 million
- Guided sales force to increase account base 20% - even in declining markets
- Helped to capture 7% in shipping cost savings

Key to my success is creative and empathetic selling. I place myself in my client's position, making it my mission to provide them with qualified and individualized solutions that work.

In today's intensely competitive marketplace, efficient and effective sales operations are critical to a company's success. The ultimate success of any sales operation requires a manager who can develop, implement, and optimize sales processes designed to achieve strategic corporate goals. I believe that I embody these traits as evidenced by my past performance, and I am eager to make immediate and long-lasting contributions for ABC Company.

I have enclosed my résumé to furnish you with additional details regarding my background and achievements, but since words on paper are no substitute for the value that I can offer, I would like to set up a personal meeting with you to discuss our mutual interests. May I call in a few days to do just that?

Yours very truly,

Adele Hanson

Enclosure – Résumé (2 pages)

Sales Manager. This letter's opening clearly states that the candidate has made a great contribution towards client retention. The rest of the letter supports this by addressing buying motivators such as improving the client base and increasing revenue.

123 Any Avenue
Calgary, AB T2T 2T2

Beth Moretti
• • •

403.555.1234
rosa@careerprocanada.ca

June 12, 2014

Jane Smith
Recruitment Manager
ABC Sales
123 Main Street
Calgary, AB T2T 2T2

Dear Ms. Smith;

Sales, promotion, and product marketing are all competitive and results-driven endeavours which challenge and excite me. If you are seeking a **highly accomplished sales professional** with expertise in identifying potential, nurturing key relationships, and finding creative solutions, please take a look at my qualifications.

I am an enthusiastic and effective team player with a talent for luxury sales. For the past six years, I have **maintained a 90% success rate**, or higher, at closing sales in my interior design portfolio. some of my greatest assets are identifying and capturing new accounts, overcoming obstacles, and being able to **close sales through effective presentations** and superior customer service. I am highly proficient at **communicating product value and benefits** to seal the deal.

My passion, social savvy, and **commitment to excellence** continually drive my high performance. Over the past several years, I have successfully forged new networks, engaged and connected with diverse individuals of all backgrounds, and achieved set business goals. During my time as a Sales Representative with Sales Plus, I was proficient at securing new revenue streams to **rank me in the top 5%** of regional sales representatives for two years. I also **exceeded 100% of my annual sales goals.**

My enclosed résumé provides further specifics of my related expertise and accomplishments, but as they are best explained in person, I look forward to meeting with you soon to discuss in detail. I am confident you will find me engaging, eager, and **fully capable of achieving *your* organization's sales objectives.** Thank you for your consideration.

Sincerely,

Beth Moretti
Enclosure: Résumé

• • •

Sales Professional. This older career-changer minimally references her current role as Interior Designer. An enthusiastic pitch emphasizes sales expertise with accomplishments and transferable skills through deliberately bolded statements.

TAMMY SMITH

1234 Any Street ▪ Sandy Beach, Ontario, Canada ▪ L1P 1P1
Cell: 705.555.1234 ▪ Email: tammysmith@careerprocanada.ca

http://ca.linkedin.com/in/tammysmithxx

October 16, 2014

Ms. Debbie Monte
General Manager
XYZ Community Development Corporation
1234 Helena Street
P.O. Box 1234
Midway, Ontario L1L 1L1

RE: Sustainability Coordinator, XYZ Community Development (Job ID #55555)

Dear Ms. Monte:

The role of Sustainability Coordinator requires an individual with a solid track record of successfully implementing municipal initiatives coupled with an exceptional business acumen and persuasive communication skills. I invite you to review my résumé which will provide a synopsis of my qualifications to effectively achieve the mandate of this position.

My involvement in municipal projects began in Victor, British Columbia and has continued in Ontario with key assignments in Midway and Sandy Beach. Whether steering community initiatives or driving the growth of two private businesses, I have played a key influencing role in collaboratively working with a wide variety of stakeholders to achieve success.

Allow me to highlight my involvement in municipal projects:

▪ Joined a six-person Steering Committee, partnering with the Town of Sandy Beach, residents and community groups to launch the Ted Brown Youth Centre. Currently, the team is tasked with developing a strategic plan to sustain and grow this valuable community resource.
▪ Served as a Founding Member of the Midway County Indoor Park Project, where I was influential in igniting support from the Midway community to raise funds for the permanent indoor skateboard park.
▪ Worked for a Midway Chiropractor where I developed outreach plans expanding business opportunities contributing to 200% growth; devised an educational workshop and involved the practice in community fundraising.
▪ Played the key role in devising, deploying and expanding Victor's skateboard park program after being chosen to champion a $37,000 Healthy Communities Grant. Captured $350,000 in capital funding to transform the program from an eight-week venture into a permanent outdoor skateboard park.

As the Principal of TS Marketing Group and former Co-Owner of Sandy Professional Lawn Care, I have elevated brand recognition, organized and participated in community trade shows, managed and heightened website presence and been an invited guest speaker. I am known for my contagious enthusiasm and above-average knowledge of marketing and business operations, understand the demographics of the area, and have built an extensive resource network of small business, municipal and community contacts.

I reviewed the Pillars and Themes of the Sustainability Plan and do not foresee any obstacles in achieving this mandate within the contracted 42-month timeframe. The plan's goals pertaining to the environment, local economy and quality of life are important to me as a local resident wanting to ensure a safe and solid future for my child.

In summary, I am proud of my successes and confident in my ability to successfully implement the XYZ Sustainability Plan as Sustainability Coordinator. I recommend a telephone or in-person interview at your earliest convenience so I can further engage you in my qualifications and excitement in fulfilling this challenging mandate.

Thank you for your time and consideration. I look forward to your call.

Sincerely,

Tammy Smith

Sustainability Coordinator. This self-employed professional leverages numerous municipal assignments and community initiatives to successfully position herself for a stable and permanent opportunity.

Cover Letter Strategist: Maureen McCann

Jim Stevens, B. Comm. – TECHNICAL PROJECT MANAGER

902.555.1234 | jstevens@careerprocanada.ca | http://www.linkedin.com/in/infojimstevens

July 13, 2014

Carl Logan
VP Technology
ABC Company
123 Any Street
Halifax, NS B1B 1B1

Re: Technical Project Manager

Dear Mr. Logan,

To achieve ongoing Return on Investment (ROI), companies must stay competitive and manage through rapid change. With extensive expertise in project management, a formal education in finance, and an innate ability to develop creative solutions to new challenges, I am the ideal candidate for the position of Technical Project Manager within your organization.

An innovative and competitive digital project manager, I have reduced redundancies, increased ROI, rationalized objectives, and driven projects to completion on time and on budget.

As Assistant Product Manager with Canada Post Corporation, I led a $6.2M national infrastructure upgrade project where I balanced the requirements of engineering, operations, and executive stakeholders, and ensured all business objectives, financial budgets, and timelines were met. My big picture thinking helped me to identify multiple barriers to the project and to design solutions before they became issues. Always looking for ways to reduce costs and enhance the bottom line, my goal is to exceed expectations. Through performance management, I have maximized output of key players and set the department on the path to success.

Here is a snapshot of some of my recent accomplishments:

- **Generated $4M in new revenue** creating Canada's top comparison shopping website, having created strong value to the end user and a specific and targeted sales action plan.
- **Mitigated loss of $86K,** having ensured compliance and identified errors and numerous barriers impeding multi-million dollar project completion.
- **Developed new product offering** from idea generation to pre-launch, including product road map and marketing plan. The product is now poised to deliver $55M over the next 5 years.

Offering extensive expertise in both project and product management and extensive expertise working with high profile market leaders, I submit my résumé for your perusal. I welcome the opportunity to meet with you to learn more about this exciting position and to discuss in further detail how my innovative and decisive leadership along with my technical expertise will be beneficial to your organization.

Sincerely,

Jim Stevens

Translates high level objectives and vision into implementation

Technical Project Manager. This candidate successfully creates context for the reader by including values; dollar figures are strategically included throughout the cover letter to address a potential employer's buying motivators.

Robert De Barros

123 Any Avenue ⊕ Kitchener ON N1N 1N1
519-555-1234 ⊕ debarros@CareerProCanada.ca

Candidate for...

SHIFT CONTROL TECHNICIAN

July 15, 2013

Ms. Jane Smith, Recruiter
Ontario Power Generation
123 Main Street
Kitchener, ON N1N 1N1

Dear Ms. Smith:

Ontario Power Generation's website states that it is committed to safety, its people, and its work environment. And that, when hiring a new employee, the interview team evaluates how the person fits in with corporate values. I am also committed to safety, work well with all people, and wish to make a positive impact on my workplace. Wanting to join Ontario Power in the role of Shift Control Technician, I am submitting my résumé.

I have the educational requirements, and more, that this position requires, including:
 ▹ Electrical Engineering Technician and Technologist diplomas;
 ▹ Certificates in computer hardware and software, AutoCAD, PLC; and,
 ▹ Industrial Maintenance Mechanic certificate.

I have related experience with electrical installation, repairs, and instrumentation; with assembly, disassembly, and modifications; with troubleshooting, preventive maintenance, and resolving technical problems through inspection and using maintenance equipment; and with PLC control systems. I am also knowledgeable in security systems operations.

In addition, I consider myself an excellent employee: dependable, as demonstrated by my 100% attendance record; safety conscious, demonstrated by a 100% safe record; and a good corporate citizen who gets along with all coworkers. I am conscientious in my day-to-day efforts, a friendly and collaborative team player, and go above and beyond to make sure I am thorough and consistent in delivering excellent work.

Your consideration of my application is appreciated. I welcome the opportunity of a personal interview.

Sincerely,

Robert De Barros
Encl: 2 pages

Technician. This recent immigrant makes a connection to the company's corporate values in the opening of his letter. Note the use of "Candidate for..." in the header, to creatively state the job title when he has not performed that exact role previously.

Cover Letter Strategist: Maureen McCann

ConnieHopkins — Web Technology Product Manager

OPTIMIZING PERFORMANCE & PRODUCT INNOVATION

July 6, 2014

Christopher Young
Chief Technology Officer
XYZ Company
123 Any Street
Toronto, ON M1M 1M1

Re: Product Manager

Dear Mr. Young,

Web-based technology companies are always on the lookout for cool new products and services. In order to gain and sustain more users, companies need to ensure their teams work together to meet their needs and exceed their expectations.

Having been an entrepreneur for most of my career, I fully appreciate the importance of engaging employees to produce high quality products. With more than 10 years of experience in technology operations management, I am confident my contribution to your company would be a welcome addition to your thriving team. I therefore submit my résumé for your perusal, demonstrating my qualifications for the position of Product Manager.

As co-founder of a web-technology start-up, I identified a market opportunity, developed and launched a product, cultivated demand, established reputation and brand, then successfully sold the product to an industry-leading giant. Being well known and respected in the local start-up community, I have an excellent understanding of user needs and am adept at translating these requirements into tangible results.

I create environments that maximize creativity, engage employees, and improve productivity. Being attuned to the needs of designers, developers, and consumers, I work proactively to design solutions that fit the needs of my customers, and am often the first to bring these solutions to market, giving a clear advantage over competitors. For these reasons, I am confident you will find me ideally suited for the position of Product Manager with your company.

When hiring employees, I look for commitment, reliability, and loyalty – and these are the qualities I offer your organization. I welcome the opportunity to meet with you in person to learn more about this exciting position and to discuss my experience in further detail.

Sincerely,

Connie Hopkins
Enclosed: Résumé

(416) 555.1234 ➲ conniehopkins@careerprocanada.ca ➲ www.linkedin.com/in/infochopkins

---

Technology Product Manager. This entrepreneur successfully targets a career change into a full-time position by honing in on a large organization's basic needs: employee engagement, productivity, and loyalty.

Amy Thompson, B.Sc. M.Sc.
Therapeutic Classification Specialist
123 Any Ave. Ottawa, ON K1K 1K1 ▪ 613-555-1234
athompson@careerprocanada.ca ▪ http://www.linkedin.com/in/athompsontcs

August 2, 2013

Ms. Jane Smith
Assistant Deputy Minister
ABC Government Department
123 Main Street
Ottawa, ON K1K 1K1

Reference: ABC Government Department, Therapeutic Classification Specialist # ABC-001-002

Dear Ms. Smith:

This letter is in response to the internally advertised assignment at ABC Government Department. As you will see in my enclosed résumé, I have extensive experience in the therapeutic classification of drugs, and Canadian therapeutic products.

As a skilled therapeutic classification specialist within ABC, I offer more than twelve years direct experience. My knowledge also includes eight years working within the drug approval process. The clinical, safety, and efficacy assessment process has been my area of expertise for the past eighteen months.

Some of my recent accomplishments in the role of therapeutic classification specialist include:

Experience as a manager - For more than five years, I have developed twelve committed staff members to deliver on extremely tight deadlines. My team continues to excel; providing increasingly improved service to internal and external clients.

Experience in drug process approval - As an integral part of the clinical, safety, and efficacy assessment team, I have extensive expertise in science-based, risk-benefit review. My strengths lie in understanding and streamlining complex data.

Experience in drug-related environments - My comprehensive understanding of the Canadian therapeutic products sector includes analysing, classifying, and researching incoming drug submissions. This includes new drug submissions, supplemental and abbreviated new drug submissions, and drug identification number (DIN) applications.

Having written for multiple medical publications, I appreciate the importance of clear communication – especially in a managerial role. Superiors, colleagues, and customers have regularly acknowledged my people management talents and significant expertise in relational databases.

Although my present role has been stimulating and fast-paced, at this point in my career I am exploring new and interesting challenges where my drug related expertise can be fully utilized. I welcome a personal meeting to discuss your requirements and my background in much greater detail.

Sincerely,

Amy Thompson
Enclosed: Résumé

Therapeutic Classification Specialist

Therapeutic Classification Specialist. This candidate effectively responded in a concise way to a very detailed "experience" requirement that included drug process approval, managerial experience, and experience in a drug related environment.

Cover Letter Strategist: Gabrielle LeClair

Jane Smith

Victoria BC, Canada K0K 0K0
555-555-1234 · janesmith@careerprocanada.ca

July 10, 2014

Jim Duncan
Manager, Tourism
Travel British Columbia
555 Mountain Road West
Victoria BC, K0K 0K0

Dear Mr. Duncan,

Thank you for taking the time to speak with me last Tuesday with respect to my job search. I appreciate the insights that you shared with me, and I was most excited to learn of your future opening for a Tourism Marketing Coordinator. After familiarizing myself with Travel BC's programs and initiatives, I am confident that my seven years of broad-based experience in marketing and communications for the tourism industry makes me an ideal candidate for this role.

As you may recall from our conversation, I have built innovative marketing and communications initiatives which increased brand awareness across Canada and the USA. As such, I am well poised to manage media and communications projects on behalf of Travel British Columbia.

I have managed special events and conferences with up to 600 attendees, including the International Travel and Tourism Conference, working collaboratively with senior management and outside consultants to design programming and secure speakers. I personally oversaw the marketing and advertising, utilizing my exceptional planning and organizational skills to reach international audiences.

The following are a small sampling of my career achievements:

· Increased brand visibility, securing a three-year sponsorship deal for the Canadian Chamber of Commerce.
· Led teams of 10, mentoring and motivating team members through collaboration.
· Achieved the number one brand among Canadian hoteliers, as measured by Cormex Research.
· Reduced costs by 50%, maintaining exceptional public relations services to 40 franchisees.

The enclosed résumé contains additional examples of the successes I have secured on behalf of my previous employers. It would be an honour to meet with you and talk in more detail about all that I offer Travel BC. I will be in contact early next week to schedule a meeting for us to discuss this opportunity further.

Sincerely,

Jane Smith
Enclosure: Résumé

Tourism Marketing Coordinator. This letter follows up on an unadvertised opportunity. The candidate reminds the recipient of a previous networking cold-call conversation and provides detailed information as to her qualifications.

9
Best
Cover Letter
Samples

Senior-Level
& Executive

Cover Letter Strategist: Lynda Reeves

DANIEL VALE, CGA

123 Any Avenue, Saskatoon, SK S1S 1S1
C: 306.555.1234 ♦ H: 306.555.2345
E: dvale@CareerProCanada.ca

BOARD & BUSINESS EXECUTIVE

June 30, 2013

Ms. Jane Smith
Human Resources Manager
ABC Association
123 Main Street
Saskatoon, SK S1S 1S1

Re: Board Director

Dear Ms. Smith,

I have a reputation for driving outstanding success as a corporate executive and not-for-profit leader in Saskatchewan. My active involvement in diverse areas and attention to current events in this province further ensure that I have what you are seeking in a highly effective **Board Member**.

Known for my business acumen and skilled negotiations, I aggressively pursue opportunities affecting a range of stakeholders. Whether collaborating with community representatives, the general public, labour, or government officials, I provide innovative ideas, comprehensive data, and build lasting relationships that make a difference. Colleagues view me as a problem-solving professional with utmost integrity who supports and encourages open dialogue.

Here is an outline of where I see my skills and background aligned with your board accountabilities:

- **Previous Board Expertise:** Appointed, recruited, or invited to assume executive roles on boards for corporations, not-for-profit entities, industry associations, and crown investments.
- **Business and Financial Management:** As controller, president, and director, managed diverse accountabilities in all sectors.
- **Corporate Governance:** Implemented governance programs in business and non-profits that brought structure and ensured compliance through more than 30 years.
- **Partnerships & Affiliations:** Established business partnerships, collaborated with ministry representatives on blended initiatives, and spawned joint community projects.
- **Organizational Development:** Devised and introduced *modus operandi* for corporations and non-profit agencies. Created, and assisted in the implementation of, many *pro forma* business plans.
- **Union Negotiation:** Averted several potential strikes in a multi-union environment and secured labour buy-in for contract agreements in every instance.

In the attached résumé are examples of achievements on various boards and in business. Next week, I will call to ensure that you have had the opportunity to review that document and to see if we can meet in the near future to discuss this in more detail.

Sincerely,

Daniel Vale

Enc. Résumé

Powerful Decision-Making ♦ Relationship Diversity ♦ Governance & Compliance

Board Director. This semi-retired candidate successfully detracts from his age. He lists a number of high-end, connectable achievements in a rich and varied career that positions him well to participate on a number of boards.

ENERGY
EXPERTISE
ETHICS

Mike Tang, MBA

123 Any Avenue ▪ Edmonton, Alberta ▪ T2T 2T2 ▪ 403.555.1234
mtang@careerprocanada.ca ▪ http://www.linkedin.com/in/mtmtang

July 15, 2013

Ms. Jane Smith
ABC Recruitment
123 Main Street
Edmonton, Alberta T1T 1T1

Position Number: CEO-123-45

Dear Ms. Smith:

Thank you for introducing me to your firm and the exciting new opportunity for a talented Chief Executive Officer at ABC Energy, which you indicated would be an ideal match for me.

I was very pleased to learn about this role, and as promised, I am following up with a copy of my résumé and executive biography. I trust this will highlight how my talents as a leader within the Oil and Gas Sector dovetail perfectly with the competencies you are seeking for the role of Chief Executive Officer.

Here is a snapshot of my experience and how it relates directly to the opportunity with ABC Energy:

ENERGY – With a forward thinking philosophy, I have delivered operational and financial excellence in the energy, oil, and gas sector. In the last ten years, I have brought a fledgling organization to year-over-year increases, making them one of the largest and most profitable drillers in Canada.

EXPERTISE - I recognize that a top-performing team is key to attaining organizational goals. By leveraging the best in our industry and delegating tactical responsibilities to the right personnel, I have successfully executed leading-edge strategies even in the face of adversity within the industry.

ETHICS - A great part of my success is based on the fact that I am a natural relationship builder who models ethics, integrity, and transparency. Having provided leadership to geographically dispersed divisions, I have built teams that have driven bottom-line objectives.

Equipped with a Masters of Business Administration and a proven track record in the energy, oil, and gas sector, I believe I have all the attributes you require to bring me forward to your client, ABC Energy. Although the job posting you forwarded requested salary information, at this time my primary goal is to learn more about the position and ensure that this role is a suitable match for my talents. Therefore, I would be very pleased to discuss my remuneration when the appropriate opportunity arises.

I look forward to the next step in this process. In the meantime, thank you for your interest and serious consideration.

Best regards,

Mike Tang, MBA
Enclosures: Résumé and Biography

"Bottom-line results through energy, ethics, and expertise"

Chief Executive Officer. This executive is writing in response to a request by a recruiter. The theme of "energy, expertise, and ethics" creates a consistent message – from tagline through to footer.

Cover Letter Strategist: Sharon Graham

JTEVEN JNOW
CHIEF EXPLORATION OFFICER
Expertly mobilizing exploration, prospecting and mining resources.

July 22, 2013

Mr. John Smith
President & CEO
ABC Resources
123 Main Street
Vancouver, BC V1V 1V1

Dear Mr. Smith:

I am writing this letter at the recommendation of your colleague Jack Arthur, CEO of Forest Services. Jack suggested that it would be mutually beneficial for us to meet, as I have recently completed a very successful assignment overseeing research in the Yukon Territory.

A professional geologist with over fifteen years experience in the mining industry, I have produced impressive results for my clients, and I am now ready to explore opportunities in organizations such as yours. Having led projects across North America, I bring extensive experience and knowledge related to the exploration and mining industry.

With most of the last ten years spent in the Northwest Territories, Yukon, Nunavut, and BC, I have established highly effective working relationships with leaders in the local First Nations, federal, provincial, and territorial governments, and other regulatory bodies. An appointed member of the BC Mineral Advisory Board and currently active with the Yukon Prospectors Association, I advise various policy and decision makers on best practices. Therefore, it would be mutually advantageous for us to delve into some of these areas of my background:
- Exploring and developing precious metal deposits across North America.
- Leading the production of two separate nickel-mining properties.
- Overseeing the permitting of the $1.8 billion ABC Creek project.
- Consulting with Canada's leading geo-environmental organizations.

I see ABC Resources as a rapidly growing company, focused on mineral discoveries in a dynamically evolving industry. Although my résumé outlines my range of projects and successful outcomes, a personal meeting would allow us to have a two-way conversation. It would be a pleasure to meet with you to develop our business relationship, share insight into our ever-changing industry, and learn more about how I can help ABC Resources to attain its objectives.

I will call you next week to set a time for us to meet in person. If you prefer to contact me sooner, please feel free to e-mail me at snow@careerprocanada.ca and I will reply without delay.

Sincerely,

Stephen Snow, B.Sc., P.Geo.

Enclosure: Résumé

123 Any Ave. Dawson, YT Y1Y 1Y1▪ P: 867-555-1234 ▪ E: snow@careerprocanada.ca

Chief Exploration Officer. By leading in with the name of a mutual contact, the candidate makes an immediate connection. His bullet points address areas where he can set the employer apart from the competition.

Rene Hunt, B.Comm, CGA

Chief Financial Officer

Transformative Financial & Operational Leadership

May 16, 2013

Mr. John Smith, President & CEO
ABC Engineering Inc.
123 Main Street
Saskatoon, SK S1S 1S1

Dear Mr. Smith,

Thank you for taking my call yesterday. I am pleased to follow up by forwarding my résumé in application for your advertised role of Chief Financial Officer.

In the past, financial executives focused on raising capital and instituting controls. Today, an effective CFO must be much more than a financial manager. As ABC Engineering Inc.'s new Chief Financial Officer, I offer expertise as a transformative change leader, strategic business partner, and administrative operations manager.

From our brief conversation, I understand that ABC is ready to move out of "recessionary mode." Change is exciting – and my specialty is effecting change and positioning organizations to improve profitability. Each new initiative is an opportunity which, if managed well, can produce outstanding results. By ensuring that accounting standards are met, instituting benchmarking, streamlining operations, and effectively managing the evolution, I carefully balance risk and reward.

However, the true value of my contribution is found in my leadership ability. A respected and inspirational leader, I put great effort into addressing the needs of all stakeholders. I thrive on challenges found in high stress situations and use a calm, analytical approach to secure commitment, trust, and support from all involved.

A lifelong learner, I believe in continuous growth. In addition to my Certified General Accountant and Bachelor of Commerce credentials, I am currently in pursuit of a Master's degree in Business Administration.

Mr. Smith, I have the background and proven capabilities to positively effect financial and operational business change to support ABC's strategic direction. Next week, I will follow up to ensure you have read my résumé and to inquire about scheduling an in-person meeting.

Thank you in advance for your serious consideration.

Respectfully,

Rene Hunt

cc. Ms. Jennifer Black, Human Resources Manager

123 Any Ave., Saskatoon, SK S1S 1S1 ▪ Telephone: 306.555.1212 ▪ Mobile: 306.555.1313 ▪ Email: rh@careerprocanada.ca

Chief Financial Officer. In the body of the letter, this "transformative" leader expressly discusses change management strategies that will bring the organization out of a tough economic situation.

ANDREW PATEL, MCS
CHIEF INFORMATION OFFICER

123 Any Avenue, Charlottetown, PE C1C 1C1 ◀▶H: 902.555.1234 ◀▶ C: 902.555.2345
apatel@careerprocanada.ca ◀▶ http://www.linkedin.com/in/apatelvptech

March 12, 2013

Mr. John Smith
President & CEO
ABC Canada
123 Main Street
Charlottetown, PE C1C 1C1

Re: Chief Information Officer

Dear Mr. Smith:

ABC Canada is a world-leading call centre operation offering a state-of-the-art telecommunications infrastructure to global Fortune 500 organizations. From our recent discussion at the Enlighten Technology Forum, I understand that you are tapping the market for a visionary information technology leader who will ensure that your organization remains at the forefront. I am such a leader and you will discover that the attached résumé expresses many values that we share.

A lifelong resident of Prince Edward Island, I offer over fifteen years of experience leading technology initiatives in call centre operations. My reputation for excellence has been earned in massive, leading-edge undertakings for some of the major players in our industry. Most recently, as Vice President of Technology, I led a key expansion and integration of an acquisition that created the second largest call centre in the region.

Bilingual in English and French, I am a powerful team leader and negotiator who inspires commitment and dedication to ongoing evolution. I meet strategic and tactical objectives by inspiring our technology project teams to deliver complex IT-related business programs while maintaining a strong bottom-line by reducing capital spend, streamlining business processes, and leveraging existing technology whenever possible.

The competencies and expertise that I offer span such diverse areas as:

▶ Executing Strategic Plans   ▶ Enterprise Project Leadership   ▶ Regulatory Compliance
▶ Managing Profit & Loss   ▶ Mergers & Acquisitions   ▶ Corporate & IT Governance
▶ Pioneering Technologies   ▶ Accelerated Resource Usage   ▶ Security & Risk Management

If you are looking for an effective CIO, you have found your match. There is much more I could say about my background, skills, and style. I would be pleased to meet with you again to enlarge on the points that we discussed at the forum and that are listed here.

Sincerely,

Andrew Patel, MCS   Enclosure: Résumé

State-of-the-art technology and telecommunications leadership for the call centre industry.

Chief Information Officer. The opening of the letter reminds the reader of a recent chance meeting at an industry event. Then, this leader hones in on his career and life in Prince Edward Island to show targeted achievements in the region.

MARK MARCH, MBA

123 Any Avenue
Oakville, Ontario L1L 1L1

Residence: (905) 555-1234
mmarch@careerprocanada.ca

June 15, 2013

Mr. John Smith
President & COO
ABC Recruitment
123 Main Street
Toronto, Ontario M1M 1M1

Dear Mr. Smith,

This letter is in response to your search for an executive with proven expertise in varied upper management roles in both the Finance and IT sectors. My experience and verifiable accomplishments match those mentioned and more. As detailed in the enclosed résumé, I have held positions from Senior Management and Vice President through Chief Operating Officer encompassing Human Resources, IT and Finance departments. My successes range from projects of significant proportions saving companies millions of dollars to guiding organizations through mergers and complete corporate restructurings.

The results I drive are accomplished with thorough planning, teamwork, conflict resolution, sensitivity, empathy and the capability to remain calm during intense crises. With a foundation of indisputable ethics and empathy for the concerns and fears in the face of immense change, I engage personnel and clients alike with sincerity and respect, employing humour appropriately to diffuse tension.

Boards of Directors, peers and company employees appreciate my efforts in addressing the human element while ensuring organization-wide revitalization with systems integration. Vigorously, and with utmost integrity, I champion change processes for optimal results in the tightest of timeframes. Meeting problems head on and through consensus building, I have launched such enterprising solutions as:

- Order entry websites including online credit card processing, fraud prevention and freight quoting
- International employee benefits programs
- Transborder logistics service
- Employee performance management system and recruiting strategies

At the moment, my salary is in the $150K range. I am flexible on the actual figure of my next role, depending on the total compensation and remuneration offered.

Mr. Smith, I have the ability to positively affect any endeavours or substantial changes, which the company in question may be facing. I look forward to an interview, which will allow me to share my background in greater detail and to discuss how I can be a positive force in any organization. I can be reached at my home most evenings. If I have not heard from you within the next week, I shall contact you to arrange the next steps in this process.

Sincerely,

Mark March

Enc. Résumé

Chief Operating Officer. Rather than offering his salary expectation as was requested by the advertisement, this candidate reveals his current salary. To encourage an interview, he suggests that he is flexible regarding future compensation.

Cover Letter Strategist: Sharon Graham

 Leadership through strategic Marketing and effective Communications.

Lynda M. Curtis
Marketing Communications Leader

May 8, 2013

Mr. John Smith
Principal Consultant
ABC Executive Search
123 Main Street
Halifax, NS B1B 1B1

Dear Mr. Smith,

I am writing to you upon the recommendation of Mark Cash, whom you recently placed in ABC Organization. I understand that your executive search firm specializes in recruiting and placing high-profile marketing and sales management professionals. As a results-oriented Marketing and Communications Leader with a drive for excellence, I can provide one of your clients with the competitive advantage required to maximize their bottom line.

During my career, I have championed and introduced a range of marketing and communication strategies that ultimately led my organization to be named as one of *Canada's Top 50 Best Managed Companies.*

- **Vision:** Unlocking market and consumer insights to enable pragmatic, results-focused marketing approach.
- **Leadership:** Spearheading projects with an inclusive management style to ensure that all stakeholder needs are met.
- **Marketing:** Contributing to the Canadian branding and advertising rollout for a $1.2 billion industry leader.
- **Communications:** Establishing a comprehensive public relations campaign positioning Canada as the industry leader.

With more than 10 years of experience working with companies throughout North America and overseas, I am a trusted advisor to top executives with a plethora of proven best practices in marketing communications. Following are actual business results to which I have contributed over the last five years.

	2005	2006	2007	2008	2009
% Over Target	100%	110%	115%	113%	105%

I am confident that my proven talents and history of driving innovative and business-focused solutions will be of considerable interest to those you represent. To that end, I think we have a mutually beneficial reason to meet.

I will contact you in the next few days to explore meeting arrangements. If you would like to have copies of my one-page profile, more detailed descriptions of some key initiatives, or my brief PowerPoint presentation, please let me know.

Looking forward to connecting with you.

Sincerely,

Lynda Curtis

Enclosed: Résumé

123 Any Avenue, Halifax , NS B1B 1B1
902-555-1234 | lmc@careerprocanada.ca | http://www.linkedin.com/in/lmc123

Communications and Marketing Leader. This marketing pro accentuates three words throughout - Leadership, Marketing, and Communications. She leads in with a recommendation and further captures attention with a chart.

Construction Project Manager

Abdulakir (Abe) Mohammad, B.E. Civil Engineering

January 9, 2013

Mr. John Smith
Canada Recruitment
123 Main Street
Toronto, ON M1M 1M1

Dear Mr. Smith,

Managing construction projects from development to delivery are my professional drivers!

As you can see from my résumé and project list, I have extensive hands-on experience as a Senior Project Engineer managing construction projects from inception to completion. I have been involved in projects varying from the smallest works to $50 million projects, covering all aspects of commercial, industrial, and civil works.

As an accomplished Civil Engineer with many years of practical construction experience, I have developed expertise in co-ordinating, managing, engineering, and contracting for the construction of new facilities and the upgrading of existing facilities. You will see that I offer an impressive record of consistently meeting plans, deadlines, budgets, and project completion, which is validated by many direct endorsements from my employers, clients, and contractors on my LinkedIn account: http://www.linkedin.com/in/abemoproject.

For the last three years, I have worked under contract as Executive Director of Projects for Al ABC, a major international developer based in the UAE. Reporting directly to the CEO, I managed the development of a number of flagship construction projects from feasibility through to commissioning and handover. I am proud to say that I was part of a top calibre team and, because of our collaborative emphasis on quality and excellence, ABC was among the first companies in the region to achieve the ISO 9001 certification.

I am a strong team manager who will interact positively with clients, contractors, labourers, and consultants to provide the highest level of support and service. Paramount to my philosophy is creating a 'cohesive project team' environment in which all stakeholders focus on a common goal.

In Toronto's multi-cultural, competitive construction market, property development companies rely on innovative professionals who bring global experience to keep them at the leading edge. Fully eligible to work in Canada as a Permanent Resident, I am certain that when you bring my résumé forward to your clients, they will see great value from meeting me in person. Therefore, I respectfully request an opportunity to discuss, in detail, my candidacy for appropriate construction project management opportunities.

Thank you for reviewing this information; I appreciate your consideration.

Sincerely,
Abe Mohammad, B.E. Civil Engineering

Enclosures/

123 Any Avenue, Toronto, ON M1M 1M1 | Canada 647.555.1234 | Dubai – UAE: +97123456789
E-Mail: abe@careerprocanada.ca | http://www.linkedin.com/in/abemoproject

Construction Project Leader. This new immigrant refers the recruiter to LinkedIn for his overseas endorsements. The closing deals with any perceived obstacles by stressing his multi-cultural experience and eligibility to work in Canada.

DAVID CHANG

123 Any Avenue, Vancouver, BC V1V 1V1   dchang@careerprocanada.ca   604.555.1234

ABC Entertainment Inc.   February 23, 2014
Suite 111, 123 Main Street
Vancouver, British Columbia   V1V 1V1

Attention: Ms. Jane Smith, President
Re: **In-house Corporate Counsel** employment opportunity

Dear Ms. Smith:

I am an experienced, senior Attorney who has spent over twenty years getting to know the interactive video entertainment industry. I balance an assertive attitude with a sincere desire to mentor my staff to achieve outstanding results on the issues we address. My solid combination of legal insight and negotiation skills has enabled me to handle many different problems confidently, and to provide sensible advice to my clients. When I first spotted the In-house Corporate Counsel opportunity on the Internet, I immediately thought, "This job would be exciting, challenging – a great opportunity to further improve my skills and knowledge in the video entertainment industry."

With a long history of experience in all of the requisite areas, I have a solid grounding in the essential skills that you expect from your In-house Corporate Counsel. I would bring to ABC Entertainment Inc. the following key strengths:

- A penchant for leadership.
- A passion for constant, continual learning.
- A talent for building harmonious, "win-win" relationships in an adversarial environment.
- Superior communication skills.
- A conscious sense of respect for everyone's efforts in the legal arena.
- The energy required to juggle high-pressure, simultaneous projects.

Although I am currently an American citizen, under NAFTA I qualify for an annually renewable Canadian work permit. I am eligible to receive a permit to act as a Foreign Law Practitioner in British Columbia and, as such, I would be licensed to advise on California and U.S. federal law. Also, I will soon be receiving a Certificate of Qualification (from the National Committee on Accreditation at the University of Ottawa) verifying that I am the equivalent of a Canadian law graduate and, ultimately, eligible to join the Law Society of British Columbia.

Thank you for reading my curriculum vitae. I am very excited to begin discussing how I could use my substantial legal expertise in service of ABC Entertainment Inc., willing to travel on business (when necessary), and happy to relocate to Greater Vancouver for the right opportunity. I will contact you in one week to discuss the status of my application; in the meantime, please feel free to call me at any time. I look forward to meeting with you soon!

Sincerely,

David Chang

Enclosures 2 (résumé, list of representative transactions)

Corporate Counsel. After going through bulleted strengths, this letter explicitly addresses the candidate's qualifications and employability. The strategy alleviates concerns that this expatriate might not be legally entitled to work in Canada.

JUBAIR A PROMERO, MBA
Global IT Services Executive

Skype: infojpro | jpro@careerprocanada.ca | www.linkedin.com/in/infojpro

Chief Executive Officer | Country Manager | General Manager | Managing Director

July 6, 2014

Susan de Freitas
Director of International Sales
XYZ Company
123 Any Street
Ottawa ON K1K 1K1

Dear Ms. de Freitas,

From researching organizations where I believe my expertise will have greatest impact, XYZ Company stands apart. This letter is to introduce myself and to offer you some background information that you may find intriguing. I believe that it would be of mutual benefit for you and I to meet and talk more about what I may be able to do for you now or at some point in the future.

I am well aware of the dynamic presence that XYZ Company has in Saudi Arabia as well as Canada. In the next few months, I will be relocating to Ottawa. It would be a privilege to meet with you there or with a member of your executive team here in Saudi - whichever is more convenient for you.

Across the years, I have built and led world-class, cross-functional teams of more than 100, and championed initiatives that consistently exceeded corporate - and customer - expectations. I have been accountable for profit and loss of multiple business divisions representing revenues in excess of $500M CDN.

A recognized results-oriented leader, I possess a strong track record of performance in high-paced organizations like XYZ Company. I also have a reputation as someone with superior interpersonal skills, and am known for resolving multiple and complex issues, whether across divisions or externally.

My résumé is enclosed. If you would like to have other items from my formal career portfolio - such as my short PowerPoint presentation, one-page biography, or selected samples of other accomplishments - please email me at jpro@careerprocanada.ca. If you prefer to speak with me in person, you can connect with me by Skype at infojpro or call me in Saudi Arabia at 00 555 12345678. If I have not heard from you in a few weeks, I will attempt to reach you to see if you have any questions about my résumé or what else I have to offer.

Sincerely,

Jubair Promero

~ Technology Leadership and Vision plus Proven General Management Expertise ~

Innovative strategies driving business success

Country Manager. This candidate exploits international experience and shows an understanding of the company's presence overseas. The closing paragraph encourages the reader to request further information.

133

JAY JACKSON, MBA

jj@careerprocanada.ca ➲ 403.555.1234 ➲123 Any Ave. Calgary, AB T2T 2T2

TRANSFORMATIONAL MANUFACTURING OPERATIONS EXECUTIVE

March 1, 2013

Mr. John Smith
President & COO
ABC Recruitment
123 Main Street
Calgary, Alberta T2T 2T2

Re: Director of Manufacturing Operations

Dear Mr. Smith:

Many Canadian manufacturing operations have taken a beating during what can now be described as a most demanding global economic recession. Organizations are challenged by tightening budgets while requiring significant changes to transform and drive them towards a better future. Accepting this challenge takes fortitude, foresight, and innovation – this is where I excel.

ABC Recruitment has a reputation for bringing proven leadership to organizations that are ready to surpass their competition. Therefore, it seems that I would be an excellent fit for your client base.

It is my belief that steadfast, positive leadership is the only way to ensure that manufacturing operations succeed. Armed with a proven history of transforming operations through foresight and innovation, I empathize with both business issues and personal sensitivities. I understand budgetary constraints and how businesses need to redefine and streamline their operations to deliver cutting-edge and cost effective initiatives – all the while maintaining strong employee buy-in. My résumé outlines examples of how I have achieved this time and again.

Here is a snapshot of the value I have delivered and that I can duplicate for your manufacturing clients:

➲ **Building** a world-class manufacturing operation and enhancing all key performance indicators.

➲ **Mentoring** department heads on team building strategies, improving retention and safety scores.

➲ **Streamlining** and converting a struggling facility, ultimately delivering 110% against output targets.

➲ **Implementing** a $5 million production process upgrade on time and under budget.

➲ **Attaining** new production records during the most difficult time in Canadian manufacturing history.

With a focus on out-performing the competition, my personal mandate is to bring and keep my organization's ranking at the top – regardless of the challenges ahead. Next week, I will contact you to arrange our first meeting so that we can delve further into my background and abilities. In the interim, if you would like more information I can forward a complete portfolio package for your convenience.

Sincerely,

Jay Jackson, MBA

Enclosures (Executive Résumé and Professional Biography)

...transforming operations through foresight and innovation

Director of Manufacturing. It is no secret that Canadian manufacturing organizations were hit hard during the recession. This executive focuses on the future in every paragraph. His bulleted achievements do not veer from his value proposition.

January 10, 2013

Mr. John Smith
Vice-President, Operations
ABC Company
123 Main Street
Toronto, Ont. M1M 1M1

Dear Mr. Smith:

I would like to be your next **Director of Operations,** a position I saw advertised on January 5 in the *Toronto Star.* The attached résumé documents 8 years' managerial and related employment, including 5 years' packaging experience. My résumé shows how I:

- Increased profits by researching costs and negotiating with customers.
- Slashed expenses by automating manual tasks.
- Motivated staff to work harder and better.
- Liaised with senior managers and executives of major corporations.

In this letter, I would like to give you an idea of the kind of person I am and how it affects the way I work. For example, when I prepared a catalogue for Bell Canada Enterprises, I liaised cooperatively with several staff, including an artist. Because the catalogue was my idea, I had supervisory responsibility; but I determined quickly that the artist was both talented and trustworthy. After letting him know what I expected of him, I gave him lots of freedom, knowing that if he had ownership in the process, he would do a much better job.

The more I observed, the more my initial impression was confirmed. My faith in the artist drew out his abilities, and both of us had the satisfaction of watching him produce excellent graphics.

This team-oriented approach is not only typical of my behaviour as an employee, but predates my entry into the work force. I started training as a hockey player when I was only 12. My coaches impressed upon me the importance of putting the team ahead of personal aggrandizement. As a result, I focused on passing and setting up goals, instead of scoring. I thus earned the respect of not only my teammates and fans but also many opponents.

I am convinced this attitude was an important factor in enabling me to win several awards, including the Canadian *Order of Merit,* and to participate on several award-winning teams. It is in this spirit that I seek to join your highly-reputed organization. Please call to set a convenient time to meet, so that we can discuss how I might best serve your enterprise.

Sincerely yours,

Charles Irving Gallagher

G

CHARLES IRVING
GALLAGHER

123 Any Avenue

Toronto, Ont.

M1M 1M1

Canada

(905) 555-1234

Director of Operations. An innovative design and layout garner interest for this candidate. The bullet points succinctly summarize relevant achievements. The candidate capitalizes on hockey experience to show a team-oriented approach.

Cover Letter Strategist: Sharon Graham

JENNY NG, MBA, CMA

Enterprise Risk Management Executive

123 Any Avenue ▪ Vancouver, BC ▪ V1V 1V1 ▪ C: 604.555.1212 ▪ jng@careerprocanada.ca

Hand Delivered / Executive Office

February 14, 2013

Mr. John Smith
President & CEO
ABC Global Corporation
Executive Office
123 Main Street
Vancouver, BC V1V 1V1

Re: VP, Enterprise Risk Management

Dear Mr. Smith:

The very recent financial crisis combined with wide-ranging security issues, information piracy, identity theft, and other global concerns have driven outrage and action from ethical and progressive organizations. I am a proven leader in the Enterprise Risk Management field seeking to connect for a peer-to-peer discussion on how I can support ABC Global Corporation's current and future needs in this area.

ABC Global Corporation has surfaced in my market research as a prime opportunity where my talents in delivering operational, financial, and legal risk management might best be applied. As an Enterprise Risk Management expert and Certified Management Account with a Master's degree in Business Administration, I offer fifteen years of experience mitigating loss. I understand the complexity of current issues and threats to organizations.

My reputation for excellence has been earned in expansive, leading-edge undertakings in Canada, the United States, and overseas. The attached résumé will reveal that I clearly possess the following competencies:

▪ STRATEGIC ENTERPRISE PLANNING – Instituted world-class security, audit, and risk management initiatives.

▪ GLOBAL LEADERSHIP – Produced a record of successes in leading international financial services organizations.

▪ CORPORATE GOVERNANCE – Established a wide range of operational frameworks and financial controls.

▪ REGULATORY COMPLIANCE – Improved communications, decreased risk, and restored accountability.

ABC Global Corporation is known for leveraging the most prominent executive talent. It is my intent to contact you within the next week to arrange for a discussion where we can explore opportunities to drive your organization's continued success. Should you require additional information, I will be pleased to forward a complete executive portfolio prior to our meeting.

Sincerely,

Jenny Ng, MBA, CMA

Enclosure / Networking Presentation on disk

Enterprise Risk Management - minimizing exposure through operational, financial and legal compliance.

Enterprise Risk Leader. The address block ensures that the executive office – and the president, in particular – receives this letter. The opening focuses on current events and the complete letter attests to enterprise risk management expertise.

MONICA CLARK, CMA

Executive Director   *Ethical Practices. Responsible Stewardship. Fiscal Consciousness.*

April 14, 2013

Ms. Jane Smith
Recruitment Consultant
Canada Recruitment
123 Main St.
Saskatoon, SK S1S 1S1

Re: Executive Director, ABC Association

Dear Ms. Smith,

Recent scandals involving financial and charitable organizations have influenced public perception. As a result, ethical practices, responsible stewardship, and fiscal consciousness are primary requirements for non-profit organizations. Therefore, I am pleased to contribute my expertise to ABC Association's future by applying for the role of Executive Director as advertised with your firm.

My research indicates that ABC Association is seeking a leader with credentials in business revitalization. I possess and exceed these requirements, having turned mediocre performance into bountiful outcomes for two similar organizations. I am certain that you will agree that ABC will benefit from such proven leadership that transforms organizations and fosters ongoing growth.

Enclosed you will find my résumé and biography that outlines the following key initiatives and more:

- Advised and collaborated with the Board of Directors in developing a vision, strategic plan, and 3-year tactical operational plan as a map to guide the organization's direction.
- Kept a keen focus on new funding sources and oversaw the development of Sask Association's fundraising, increasing donations by 29% in a weak economy (and in only two years).
- Spearheaded the planning, implementation, and execution of Charitable Fund's leading-edge volunteer development program.
- Instituted structures and governance to mitigate risks and judicially administer the revenue, funds, grants, expenditures, and cash flow of both Sask Association and Charitable Fund.

Personal integrity, truthfulness, transparency, and respect for diversity are of primary importance to me. As a result, I have gained respect and trust from board members, employees, donors, volunteers, public, and all stakeholders. I believe that my ability to provide direction, diffuse tension, and inspire these individuals is key to the successful outcomes I have produced.

As a financial manager, I have a deep understanding of not-for-profit accounting principles and practices. As a lifelong learner, I am currently in pursuit of my Masters in Business Administration and should be completing it by the end of the year. This credential will partner with my current designation as a Certified Management Accountant in my ongoing professional development.

With a personal commitment to leadership with ethics and integrity, responsible stewardship, and fiscal consciousness, I am confident that I am the ideal candidate for ABC's role of Executive Director. In the next week, I will contact your office to ensure that my résumé arrived, forward my complete executive portfolio, and arrange a time to meet so that you can bring me forward to ABC Association's selection committee.

Sincerely,

Monica Clark, CMA

Encl. Résumé

123 Any Ave, Saskatoon, SK S1S 1S1 ● 306.555.2345 ● mclark@careerprocanada.ca

Executive Director. In the opening paragraph, this candidate resolves a real-life business concern with her competencies. In the body, she connects the association's needs to her background and shows that she is fulfilling an MBA requirement.

Beth Armstrong, ITIL, PMP   Senior Executive - Global Technology

Eastview, AB T4T 4T4 | H: 780.555.1234 | C: 780.555.4321 | BArmstrong@careerprocanada.ca

June 28, 2014
Susanne Deschamps
Executive Recruiter
XYZ Company
123 Any Road
Calgary, AB, T0T 0T0

Re: Chief Technology Officer / Posting # 000123

Dear Ms. Deschamps:

As an experienced senior executive in technology, I have implemented IT strategy for thriving international businesses. I have recently returned to Canada after an overseas tenure and am aware if your clients' need for global leadership; I am enclosing documentation that summarizes my qualifications.

With over 15 years of experience, I offer much more than technological expertise. Having held a senior executive role in a billion-dollar corporation, I have been an instrumental contributor to all facets of corporate strategy. By applying a combination of technical and business acumen, I create a competitive advantage for the company.

Based on my research about your firm's demographics, I possess and exceed the attributes your clients seek:

- Promoted to consecutive senior executive roles with increasing responsibility and focus on IT Infrastructure and Disaster Recovery for a top ranked financial institution in North America with $5.8 billion in assets.

- Championed major IT projects supporting operations in 23 countries across Europe, Asia, Africa, as well as North and South America.

- Supported an aggressive expansion plan executing and managing the IT component, relocating 10 Canadian office locations to larger venues.

- Implemented systems and facilitated vendor selection providing local offices for a Canadian based provider in countries across the Middle East.

I am fluently bilingual in both Canadian official languages, English and French. I offer tremendous value to your Canadian-based clients wishing to expand globally or international clients seeking to solidify IT in Canadian operations. In addition to my extensive leadership experience, I possess multiple credentials in Information Technology and am a certified Project Management Professional.

It is my intent to contact you within the week to arrange for an appointment to discuss the value that I offer to you and one of your clients. In the event that you would like more information, I would be glad to forward a complete executive portfolio in preparation for our meeting.

Sincerely,

Beth Armstrong, ITIL, PMP
Enclosure: Résumé

Beth Armstrong | Global IT Solutions for a Canadian Market Place

Global IT Executive. This letter targets an executive firm using language that is appropriate for them. This candidate has done her homework and when discussing expertise, she refers to the firm's clients' needs.

SHAWN J. REDMOND, BCOMM

123 Any Street • Pickering, ON L1L 1L1 • Ph: 905.555.1234 • sjr@careerprocanada.ca

Global Sales &

S J
R

Marketing Leader

December 27, 2014

Laura Bell
Human Resources Manager
ABC Corp
55 Swan Road
Toronto, ON M1M 1M1

Re: **Global Marketing Director**

Dear Ms. Bell,

As a strategic growth and business development executive with a progressive ten-year career, I find myself eager to apply my talents to the new and challenging opportunities noted in your recent posting for a Global Marketing Director. Permit me to provide you with some insight into the expertise I offer your organization.

Currently, as International Marketing Director for Mundys International Inc., I play an integral role in leading international marketing initiatives. With global accountability, I have been instrumental in skyrocketing profit by 17% in our European division. I consistently drive sales and operational performance by combining solid marketing expertise, clear expectations, and decisive and motivational leadership to increase the bottom line.

As detailed in the attached résumé, my expertise in the following areas has resulted in generating revenue and increasing profitability:

- Global Market Development
- Brand Building & Positioning
- Consumer Research
- Sales, Marketing & Advertising
- Product Launch
- Team Development & Leadership
- P&L Management
- Competitive Market Analysis
- Business Intelligence

With a passion for networking and building long-term strategic partnerships, I empower leaders at all levels within the organization. I possess an engaging leadership style and have developed a reputation as a change agent who consistently surpasses goals. My fluency in multiple languages, including Spanish and French, has also provided me with unique business advantages.

I would welcome the opportunity to meet with you to discuss this intriguing career opportunity in more detail and to further explain why I am confident of the contributions I can make for your organization. To schedule an interview at your convenience, please do not hesitate to contact me at 905.555.1234.

Sincerely,

Shawn Redmond

Résumé Enclosed

WORLD CLASS BUSINESS DEVELOPMENT THROUGH STRATEGIC SALES & MARKETING LEADERSHIP

Global Marketing Director. A solid letter that focuses on international marketing experience and bottom-line results within Europe. The bulleted list clearly features key competencies.

123 Any Avenue
Toronto, Ontario
M1M 1M1

MARK T. HARRINGTON, MBA

Phone (416) 555-2345
Cell (416) 555-1234
E-mail mth@careerprocanada.ca

Via e-mail

January 5, 2013

John Smith
Senior Recruitment Consultant
ABC Recruitment
123 Main St.
Toronto, Ontario M1M 1M1

Re: Government Services Director – Reference 123

Dear Mr. Smith,

As a seasoned Government Services Director with a stellar record of producing results, I can offer the vision and direction required to lead your client to the next level. Anticipating your need for such leadership, I am enclosing a résumé summarizing my qualifications for your review.

As the current Director of Corporate Services within the Northern Ontario Community Centres, I have developed a thorough understanding of the government sector. My core competencies include leading the full scope of financial, human resources, administrative, systems, and facilities management units.

My proven ability to develop effective solutions to complex business challenges sets my performance apart. In my present position and throughout my career, I have played a critical role in leading organizations through a variety of major transformations. By building consensus in supporting the organization's strategic directions and effectively managing change, I have earned a verifiable reputation for consistently converting corporate strategies into tangible results.

Following are some brief highlights of the strengths and experience that I bring to the table:
- Spearheading large-scale corporate mergers and reorganizations to improve operational effectiveness.
- Working closely with Boards and Committees to identify needs and surpass all expectations.
- Understanding and acting on government agenda to obtain funding and service opportunities.
- Coaching, mentoring, and developing employees to instil a team spirit and focused direction.
- Fostering strong alliances with internal and external stakeholders to ensure customer satisfaction.
- Improving financial budgeting, reporting, and controls to effectively contain costs and manage risk.
- Streamlining business processes and utilizing appropriate technology to produce corporate efficiencies.

The key to my success is a collaborative management approach. My colleagues have characterized me as a dedicated and dependable professional with the versatility and flexibility to work effectively with diverse environments and management styles. Finally, my ongoing dedication to professional development is evident as I hold an MBA augmented by university studies in Executive Leadership, Strategic Change, Human Resources, and Information Systems.

Although my present position has been stimulating and fast-paced, at this point in my career I am confidentially exploring a new and interesting challenge where my broad expertise can be fully utilized. I welcome a personal meeting and will contact you during the week of January 12, so that we can discuss your requirements and my background further.

Thank you for your interest and consideration.

Sincerely,
Mark Harrington

Enclosure

Government Services Officer. This letter specifies the job title and reference number posted by the recruiter. The opening aptly addresses the recruiter and his client – the government. The closing reminds the reader that this is a confidential search.

CHRISTINE CLARK

PO Box 123 ▪ Exeter ON ▪ N1N 1N1 ▪ 519-555-1234 ▪ cclark@careerprocanada.ca

Applicant for: Ontario Court of Justice
                                            Justice of the Peace

July 31, 2014

Submitted through website

Recently retired after more than 30 years in nursing, the last 10 of which were served in isolated communities in Ontario, Yukon Territories and Nunavut, I apply with confidence to the role of Justice of the Peace, serving remote communities of Canada's indigenous peoples.

Having spent alternate months living in fly-in communities that numbered up to 1200, I came to understand the residents' complex challenges. I gained an appreciation for cultural norms, the impact of isolation, and for how people cope with health challenges. I know that my deep knowledge of and respect for our indigenous peoples would positively impact a judicial role.

Serving in "expanded scope nursing," during which a physician's advice was at the end of the phone rather than the end of a hall, I further developed my decisiveness, judgment, and ability to calmly assess critical situations — you will find examples of these on my résumé. The workload was heavy, often stressful, but always rewarding. With time, I earned the respect of Chiefs, elders, the extended community and physicians. I attribute this to my consistently respectful manner, open communications, and appropriate strategies.

Often the senior nurse, I mentored newly graduated nurses and, working within my employer's parameters, I improved health programming. After recognizing the negative impact that an annual dog kill exerted on community health, I launched a program to change the activity. Now in its eighth year, and expanded to a second community, the program reduced juvenile delinquent behaviour, improved safety and sanitary conditions, and engaged residents in positive change.

It would indeed be an honour to continue my service in these communities as a Justice of the Peace. I sincerely hope that I have sparked your interest in my abilities and suitability, and hope to hear from you with an invitation to an interview. In the meantime, I extend my gratitude for your time and consideration.

Yours truly,

Chris Clark

Encl: résumé

Justice of the Peace. This letter successfully transitions a retired Canadian nurse to a Justice of the Peace role. The header puts emphasis on the target position, while the body of the letter focuses on her unique background working in remote locations.

Cover Letter Strategist: Lynda Reeves

Arnie A. Powell

Toronto, ON M1M 1M1 | aapowell@careerprocanada.ca
H: 416.555.1234 | C: 416.555.4321

| Performance Turnaround & Measurement |
| Team Building & Mentoring |
| Brand & Culture Revitalization |

Operational Performance Executive

July 6, 2014

James Crawford
Recruitment Manager
ABC Organization
123 Any Road
Toronto, ON M1M 1M1

Re: VICE PRESIDENT OF OPERATIONS, LEADING CHANGE FOR RESULTS

Dear Mr. Crawford,

I enjoyed meeting you today and greatly appreciated the opportunity to talk about where ABC Organization is heading. From everything that we discussed, I feel confident that my diversity of roles and experiences will be beneficial in reaching your goals. It would be a privilege to be your Vice President of Operations, leading change for results.

Known for building, revitalizing, and mentoring powerful teams, I have become a transition specialist who establishes collaborative internal relations. I enjoy working with members of the executive and cascading information across the organization to ensure that everyone clearly understands the vision. In these ways, I secure commitment to initiatives that deliver customer-centric, revenue-generating solutions.

Throughout my career in England, I championed a number of developments which provided me with the foundation and understanding that I believe ABC Organization values. Now that I have initiated my transition to Canada, I look forward to achieving similar results for you.

Being the Vice President of Operations on your leadership team appeals to me even more since meeting with you. Thank you so much for your time and interest.

I realize that I left you with a lot to digest as you consider me for the role. If there is other information that would help in some way, I hope that you will contact me. As before, I welcome your questions and encourage you to connect with me by email (aapowell@careerprocanada.ca) or cell phone (416.555.4321) whenever you wish.

Regards,

Arnie Powell

Enclosure: Business Plan

Leading Change for Results

Operational Performance Executive. This follow-up to a previous meeting succinctly targets a change leadership role within the organization. The second paragraph focuses on leadership fit while the third focuses on organizational values.

Monica Therrien, P. ENG.

Senior Executive - International Real Estate Development & Asset Management

Whistler, BC | C: 604.555.1234 | mtherrien@careerprocanada.ca

August 15, 2014

David Macdonnell
Human Resources Manager
ABC Company
123 Any Street
Whistler, BC V1V 1V1

Dear Mr. Macdonnell:

Regardless of recent turmoil in real estate markets across North America, Canadian banks have kept a tight rein on economics by tightening regulations on new developments and property investments. As the next wave of emerging trends present themselves, it is crucial to employ the most effective leadership to seize lucrative growth opportunities. What better time for ABC Company to engage a talented real estate development and asset management executive, a veteran in the Canadian market?

Our meeting was both informative and stimulating, shedding tremendous light about your organizational needs for the role of Senior Vice President of Asset Management. Thank you for taking the time to be so explicit. Allow me to reinforce the points from our discussion with the following achievements from my past:

○ Sourced land for one of the largest shopping malls in Alberta and opened on time with over 80% occupancy. In less than one year, the occupancy rate hit 100%, initiating a ten-year expansion plan.

○ Reduced financial burden on project management teams by creating innovative cash flow strategies. This saved costs and provided project managers more time to meet deadlines.

○ Currently managing a $1.2B venture projected for completion in 2016 with 780,000 m^2 of mixed–use development. Includes 300,000 m^2 sports facility, 33,500 parking spaces, two high-end residential buildings, and 850 units for sale.

I have served Canadian organizations at home and abroad in massive global projects, I bring exceptional communication skills in English and French, and have worked collaboratively in remote areas of Northern Canada. I am a natural team leader who takes full advantage of business opportunities with an extensive network of Canadian contacts. I overcome cultural gaps, lead complex projects, and collaborate with local experts to exceed objectives.

I like the fact that your organization promotes ethical behaviour and corporate sustainability. I believe my value is all about positioning business to fulfill its objectives with integrity and I am looking forward to doing that with ABC Company in the coming years. Thank you for your serious consideration of my credentials. I welcome the next step in this recruitment process.

Sincerely,

Monica Therrien, P. Eng.

Delivering High-end Development Projects ON TIME. EVERY TIME.

Real Estate Development Executive. This follow-up letter successfully focuses on many discussion points brought up during a meeting. The candidate demonstrates a broad range of regional and international experience throughout the letter.

Cover Letter Strategist: Sharon Graham

Strategic
Human Resource
Leadership

Charlene Dove, CHRP
Senior HR Management ◀ Organizational Development ◀ Employee Relations

March 12, 2013

Mr. John Smith
Chief Executive Officer
ABC Company
123 Main Street
Fredericton, NB E1E 1E1

Dear Mr. Smith:

From my research, I understand that ABC Company has a strong and growing presence in the region. It seems that your organization is now positioned and ready to establish a full-fledged Human Resources Department. Having built a comprehensive HR infrastructure from the ground up, I believe that my background will be of great value as you take your organization towards the future.

My career in human resources management spans over ten years of leadership expertise. A Certified Human Resources Professional, my repertoire of competencies has been built in a large Human Resources organization and a number of growing organizations that are very similar to ABC Company in structure and scope.

My talents and experience driving results through people is also likely to be of great interest to you. Under my leadership, our organization has been credited with driving significant gains in:

◀ Strategic HR Leadership - Attained over ten years of experience in the full scope of strategic human resources management and support.

◀ Organizational Development - Facilitated a major organizational cultural change, introducing a business model based on teamwork, training, mentoring, and employee empowerment.

◀ Employee Relations - Enhanced employee relations and teamwork by instituting an innovative communications program focused on employee concerns and practical business needs.

◀ Recruitment and Retention - Re-engineered human resource procedures to streamline recruitment and selection, orientation, and performance management programs to improve overall retention.

◀ Compensation and Benefits - Established compensation, perquisite, and incentive programs that ensured equity, enhanced productivity, and improved employee retention.

◀ Legislative Compliance – Designed and launched a full portfolio of policies, procedures, and programs to comply with current Canadian legislation and guidelines.

As a generalist, I am best suited to start up your HR division because I have independently managed, worked, and grown the full scope of HR. As such, I have established a broad range of initiatives. More importantly, I am not afraid to "get my hands dirty" and do the hard work of administrative human resources until we are ready to expand.

Throughout my career, I have demonstrated versatility, commitment, and professionalism. My colleagues characterize me as a hardworking professional who leads with integrity. I have succeeded in every position that I have held by holding true to my core values – credibility, honesty, and empathy.

If you are seeking a results-oriented Human Resources leader, who will work alongside you to make a tangible and immediate impact, I would welcome the opportunity to explore becoming a member of your senior management team. Our collaborations will certainly lead to exciting enhancements in organizational culture and employee engagement.

Thank you for your time and professional courtesy in reviewing the enclosed résumé.

Sincerely,

Charlene Dove, CHRP

Strengthens employees, teams, and organizations through strategic human resources leadership
123 Any Ave., Fredericton, NB E1E 1E1 ◀ 506-555-1234 ◀ cdove@careerprocanada.ca ◀ http://www.linkedin.com/in/cdovehr

Human Resources Leader. This candidate creates a job opening by directly addressing the CEO and making a connection with his organization's needs. In the letter's closing, she subtly indicates that she can help him better engage employees.

Leadership stratégique en ressources humaines

Charlene Dove, CHRA
Gestionnaire senior en RH ◀ Développement organisationnel ◀ Relations avec les employés

Le 12 mars, 2013

M. John Smith
Président directeur général
Compagnie ABC
123 rue Principale
Fredericton, NB E1E 1E1

Monsieur Smith,

Selon mes recherches, je constate que la Compagnie ABC jouit d'une forte et croissante présence dans la région. Il semble que votre entreprise est maintenant prête à mettre sur pied son propre département de ressources humaines. Ayant déjà élaboré de A à Z, une infrastructure complète de ressources humaines je crois fermement que mon expérience sera des plus précieuses et vous aidera à tourner votre organisation vers l'avenir.

Ma carrière en ressources humaines est basée sur plus d'une dizaine d'années d'expertise en leadership. Je suis une professionnelle certifiée en ressources humaines et j'ai acquis mes compétences au sein d'une grosse organisation dans le domaine et auprès de plusieurs entreprises en croissance qui sont très similaires à la Compagnie ABC de par leur structure et leur envergure.

Mon talent et mon expérience à générer des résultats concrets en travaillant avec les employés seront aussi d'un grand intérêt pour vous. Sous ma direction, notre entreprise a présenté des gains significatifs en :

◀ Leadership stratégique en RH – Plus de dix années d'expérience dans toute la sphère de gestion stratégique et de support en ressources humaines.

◀ Développement organisationnel – Instauration d'un changement culturel majeur au sein de l'organisation en introduisant un modèle d'affaires basé sur le travail d'équipe, la formation, le mentorat et la valorisation des employés

◀ Relations avec les employés – Revalorisation des relations entre les employés et du travail d'équipe en instaurant des programmes innovateurs en communications ciblant les préoccupations des employés et les besoins pratiques de l'entreprise.

◀ Recrutement et rétention – Restructuration des procédures en ressources humaines afin d'uniformiser les processus de recrutement et de sélection, orientation et programmes de gestion afin d'améliorer la rétention globale et le sentiment d'appartenance des employés.

◀ Compensation et bénéfices– Compensation établie, bonus et incitatifs assurant l'équité, une productivité accrue et un meilleur taux de rétention des employés.

◀ Conformité aux lois et règles – Création et lancement d'un portfolio de politiques, procédures et programmes en conformité avec les lois et directives canadiennes en vigueur.

En tant que généraliste, je suis la candidate idéale pour implanter votre département de ressources humaines puisque j'ai travaillé, géré et vécu l'évolution de tous les aspects relatifs aux RH. J'ai ainsi mis sur pied une panoplie de projets et je n'ai surtout pas peur de « mettre la main à la pâte » et d'effectuer les tâches administratives de base nécessaires en ressources humaines afin d'assurer la pleine expansion de votre département.

J'ai fait preuve, tout au long de ma carrière, de polyvalence, d'engagement et de professionnalisme. On dit de moi que je suis une professionnelle qui travaille fort et qui dirige avec intégrité. J'ai réussi dans tous mes postes en restant fidèle à mes valeurs de base – la crédibilité, l'honnêteté et l'empathie.

Si vous êtes à la recherche d'un véritable leader en ressources humaines qui vise les résultats souhaités et qui travaillera à vos côtés afin d'en arriver à un impact immédiat et concret, je serais heureuse de faire partie de votre équipe de cadres supérieurs. Notre collaboration nous conduira très certainement à de stimulantes améliorations de la culture organisationnelle et du sentiment d'appartenance des employés.

Je vous remercie de prendre le temps de consulter mon curriculum vitae ci-joint et vous prie d'agréer, M. Smith, l'expression de mes sentiments distingués.

Charlene Dove, CHRA

Renforcer les employés, les équipes et les entreprises par un
leadership stratégique en ressources humaines

123 Ave. Quelconque., Fredericton, NB E1E 1E1 ◀ 506-555-1234
cdove@careerprocanada.ca ◀ http://www.linkedin.com/in/cdovehr

Leader en ressources humaines. Cette candidate se crée un poste en contactant le Président directeur général directement afin de cibler les besoins de son entreprise. Dans la fermeture de cette lettre, elle fait preuve d'expertise.

Cover Letter Strategist: Sharon Graham

Chris Banner, M.B.A.
Pharmaceutical Sales & Marketing Leader

123 Any Avenue, Montreal, QC H1H 1H1 | 514.555.1313 | cbanner@careerprocanada.ca | http://www.linkedin.com/in/cbpharma

April 20, 2013

Ms. Jane Smith
VP Human Resources
ABC Pharma
123 Main Street
Montreal, QC H1H 1H1

Re: Director, Sales and Marketing

Dear Ms. Smith:

In today's market, pharmaceutical organizations need effective leadership and strategies to increase profitability. If you are currently in the market for banner sales, you have found your new Director of Sales and Marketing.

With this letter, I am including a profile and some case studies that will show you how I was able to motivate my team, drive sales, and attain positive bottom-line results even in the most difficult economic market. I understand that your time is valuable, so I have also included a snapshot of my results here.

I will call you in the next few days to explore the value I can bring to ABC Pharma as a key senior manager on your team. If you require further information, please contact me at your convenience.

Regards,

Chris Banner

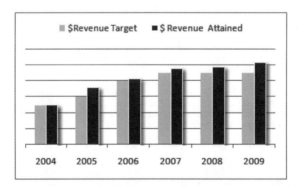

...banner sales in even the most difficult economic environments

---

Pharmaceutical Sales Leader. A picture is worth a thousand words. This highly proactive and direct leader does not waste time and energy in directing the reader to the employer's buying motivators – bottom-line results.

Chris Banner, M.B.A.
Leader en ventes et du marketing pharmaceutiques

123 Ave Quelconque, Montréal, QC H1H 1H1 | 514.555.1313 | cbanner@careerprocanada.ca | http://www.linkedin.com/in/cbpha

Le 20 avril, 2013

Mme Jane Smith
VP ressources humaines
ABC Pharma
123 rue Principale
Montréal, QC H1H 1H1

Re: Directeur des ventes et du marketing

Madame Smith,

Dans le marché actuel, les compagnies pharmaceutiques ont besoin de leadership et de stratégies afin d'accroître leur rentabilité. Si votre but est d'atteindre et de dépasser vos objectifs de ventes globales, vous venez de trouver votre nouveau directeur des ventes et du marketing.

Vous trouverez ci-joint mon profil ainsi que des études de cas qui vous montreront comment j'ai été en mesure de motiver mon équipe, de diriger les ventes et d'atteindre les objectifs de base même au sein d'une économie des plus difficiles. Je sais que votre temps est précieux, c'est pourquoi j'ai aussi ajouté ci-dessous un bref aperçu de mes résultats obtenus.

Je vous contacterai dans les prochains jours afin d'explorer ma contribution potentielle à ABC Pharma en tant que gestionnaire supérieur au sein de votre équipe. Si vous désirez de plus amples informations, veuillez communiquer avec moi à votre convenance.

En vous remerciant de votre attention,

Chris Banner

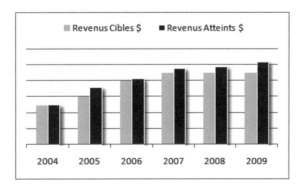

...objectifs de ventes atteints malgré les situations économiques difficiles.

Leader en ventes pharmaceutiques. Une image vaut mille mots. Ce leader, direct et proactif, ne perd pas de temps et d'énergie en dirigeant le lecteur vers les éléments motivateurs de base – des résultats clairs et nets.

Cover Letter Strategist: Sharon Graham

LEONA MARTIN, M.A (Economics)

Economic Development Officer

123 Any Avenue, Ottawa, ON K1K 1K1 ■ P: 613.555.1234 ■ C: 613.555.2345
E: lmartin@careerprocanada.ca ■ L: www.linkedin.com/in/leonamartinEDO

> Government of Canada
> Policy Development Leadership

July 28, 2013

John Smith
ABC Public Service Careers
123 Main Street
Ottawa, ON K1K 1K1

Re: JOB ID GC123 – Director of Policy Development

Dear Mr. Smith:

With over fifteen years delivering leadership to the Government of Canada in Economic Analysis, Policy Development, and Program Administration, it is my pleasure to apply for your advertised position of *Director of Policy Development*.

Completely fluent in both national languages, I offer extensive expertise in directing, organizing, controlling, and evaluating economic policy, research, and programs. My specialty is in instituting public policy, regulatory change, and innovation to support industrial and commercial business development, transportation, and public services in both urban and rural environments.

Although I am best known for economic policy development for the Government of Canada, having developed my career within two municipal agencies, my knowledge goes beyond the mechanics and delivery of programs and services that enhance economic prosperity for Canadians. The value I offer, which other candidates may not possess, is a true, deep understanding of how our decisions shape individuals and businesses in localized regions across Canada.

Armed with a passion for creating economic prosperity for Canadians through business development, I foster an entrepreneurial climate whereby new and innovative partnerships are developed and leveraged. By supporting and encouraging proactive rather than reactive strategies, I create a positive environment for business growth.

The enclosed Curriculum Vitae will corroborate that I currently have all of the key requirements listed in your job posting, so I will not repeat those here. As per your policy, for your convenience, I have also applied online through the Internal Job Posting Board on the Government of Canada's Intranet. Additionally, you will find that my reputation for overcoming insurmountable obstacles and establishing policies and programs is well documented on the Internet and in the media.

I understand that you are committed to employment equity and encourage disclosure to accommodate a disability. A car accident in my early childhood required that my right hand be amputated. As you can see from the significant achievements in my career, this has not impeded me in any way. In terms of our first interview, there is no requirement to make any accommodation, as I am fully self-sufficient. In fact, I am certain that we will focus immediately on the ways in which I may add value to the role of *Director of Policy Development* by leveraging my wealth of knowledge and experience.

Looking forward to taking the next step in your recruitment process.

Very sincerely,

Leona Martin, M.A.
Enclosure: Curriculum Vitae

■■■ Creating Economic Prosperity for Canadians through Business Development ■■■

Policy Development Leader. This leader powerfully includes added value in the third paragraph by discussing an area of experience that most other candidates clearly will not possess.

LEONA MARTIN, MA (Économie)

Agent de développement économique

| Gouvernement du Canada
| Leadership en développement des politiques |

123 Avenue Quelconque, Ottawa, ON K1K 1K1 ▪ T: 613.555.1234 ▪ C: 613.555.2345
E: lmartin@careerprocanada.ca ▪ L: www.linkedin.com/in/leonamartinEDO

Le 28 juillet, 2013

John Smith
ABC Carrières à la fonction publique
123 Principale
Ottawa, ON K1K 1K1

Re: ID EMPLOI GC123 – Directeur en développement des politiques

Monsieur Smith,

Cumulant plus de quinze années en leadership dans des postes en analyse économique, développement de politiques et administration de programmes au sein du Gouvernement fédéral, il me fait grand plaisir de proposer ma candidature pour votre poste de *Directeur en développement des politiques.*

Je suis parfaitement à l'aise dans les deux langues officielles et je vous offre une grande expertise en direction, organisation, contrôle et évaluation des programmes de politique économique et de recherche. Je suis spécialisée dans l'implantation de politiques publiques, de changements régulatoires, d'innovation et de support au développement commercial et industriel, au transport et aux services publics en milieux rural et urbain.

Bien que surtout connue pour mon travail en développement de politiques économiques pour le gouvernement du Canada, j'ai aussi œuvré au sein de deux agences municipales : mes connaissances et mon expertise dépassent donc la simple mécanique de livraison de programmes et services destinés à améliorer la prospérité financière des citoyens canadiens. J'offre une valeur que la plupart des candidats ne possèdent pas, i.e. une compréhension profonde et vraie de l'impact de nos décisions sur les individus et les entreprises en région à travers le pays.

Passionnée par la création d'une prospérité économique pour les canadiens par le développement d'affaires, je prône un climat d'entrepreneurship où on développe et supporte de nouvelles alliances innovatrices. En mettant l'emphase sur des stratégies proactives plutôt que réactives, je crée un environnement propice au développement d'affaires.

Mon curriculum vitae ci-joint vous permettra de constater que je possède toutes les qualités et aptitudes requises et énumérées dans votre offre d'emploi. Je ne les répéterai donc pas ici. Conformément à votre politique, j'ai aussi posé ma candidature en ligne via le babillard interne d'offres d'emplois sur le réseau intranet du Gouvernement du Canada. De plus, vous constaterez que ma capacité à vaincre des obstacles insurmontables et à établir de solides politiques et programmes est bien documentée sur internet et dans les médias.

Je comprends que vous pratiquez l'équité en matière d'emploi et que vous encouragez la divulgation de toute information vous permettant d'offrir un environnement adapté en cas d'handicap. J'ai été victime d'un accident de la route étant enfant et on a dû amputer ma main droite, mais comme vous pourrez le constater en consultant mon parcours de carrière, ce handicap ne m'a aucunement entravée. Il n'y a pas lieu de prendre d'arrangements particuliers pour notre première entrevue. Je suis entièrement autonome. En fait, je suis certaine que nous pourrons nous concentrer immédiatement sur ce que je peux apporter comme contribution au rôle de *Directeur en développement des politiques* en mettant mon bagage de connaissances et d'expérience à profit.

J'ai très hâte de franchir la prochaine étape de votre processus de recrutement et je vous prie d'agréer, M. Smith, l'expression de mes sentiments les meilleurs.

Leona Martin, MA
p.j.: Curriculum Vitae

▪▪▪ **La prospérité économique par le développement d'affaires** ▪▪▪

Leader en développement des politiques. Ce leader a su inclure une plus-value dans le troisième paragraphe en mentionnant une expertise que la plupart des candidats ne posséderont sans doute pas.

APPENDICES

APPENDIX A — 100 WORDS THAT ARE COMMONLY MISSPELLED IN CANADIAN COVER LETTERS

✔ Correct Spelling	✗ Incorrect Spelling
Accept (agree)	Except
Accessible	Acessible/Accessable
Accommodate	Acommodate/Accomodate
Acknowledgement	Acknowledgment
Acquire	Aquire
Analyze	Analyse
Authorized	Authorised
B.Sc. (Bachelor of Science in Canada)	B.S.
Behaviour	Behavior
Benefited	Benefitted
Calibre	Caliber
Cancelled	Canceled
Capital (city)	Capitol
Capital (money)	Capitol
Capitalize	Capitalise
Catalogue	Catalog
Categorize	Categorise
Centimetre	Centimeter
Centralize	Centralise
Centre	Center
Centred	Centered
Characterize	Characterise
Colour	Color
Computerize	Computerise
Correspondence	Correspondance
Counselled	Counseled
Counsellor	Counselor
Customize	Customise
Defence	Defense
Demeanour	Demeanor
Dual (double)	Duel
Elicit (bring about)	Illicit
Emigrate (leave a place)	Immigrate
Endeavour	Endeavor
Enrol	Enroll
Enrolment	Enrollment
Except (exclude)	Accept

APPENDIX A — 100 WORDS THAT ARE COMMONLY MISSPELLED IN CANADIAN COVER LETTERS

✔ Correct Spelling	✗ Incorrect Spelling
Familiarize	Familiarise
Fervour	Fervor
Finalize	Finalise
Focused	Focussed
Fulfill	Fulfil
Grey	Gray
Harmonize	Harmonise
Honour	Honor
Honoured	Honored
Illicit (unlawful)	Elicit
Immigrate (enter a place)	Emigrate
Initialize	Initialise
Instalment	Installment
Kilometre	Kilometer
Labelled	Labeled
Labour	Labor
Labourer	Laborer
Levelled	Leveled
Liaise	Liase
Licence (a certificate)	License
License (to allow)	Licence
Litre	Liter
Manager	Manger
Manoeuvre	Maneuver
Metre (unit of measurement)	Meter
Minimize	Minimise
Mitre	Miter
Mobilize	Mobilise
Modelled	Modeled
Mould (to shape something)	Mold
Neutralize	Neutralise
Occasional	Occassional
Occurrence	Occurance
Offence	Offense
Organization	Organisation
Organize	Organise
Paycheque	Paycheck

APPENDIX A — 100 WORDS THAT ARE COMMONLY MISSPELLED IN CANADIAN COVER LETTERS

✔ Correct Spelling	✗ Incorrect Spelling
Practice (a place)	*Practise*
Practise (to rehearse)	*Practice*
Premier (first)	*Premiere*
Premiere (grand opening)	*Premier*
Principal (head of an organization)	*Principle*
Principal (money)	*Principle*
Principle (basic truth)	*Principal*
Prioritize	*Prioritise*
Privilege	*Priviledge*
Realize	*Realise*
Recognize	*Recognise*
Reflection	*Reflexion*
Résumé / Resumé	*Résume/Resume*
Rigour	*Rigor*
Scrutinize	*Scrutinise*
Separate	*Separate*
Specialize	*Specialise*
Stabilize	*Stabilise*
Than (comparing something)	*Then*
Then (time)	*Than*
Travelled	*Traveled*
Unionized	*Unionised*
Utilize	*Utilise*
Visualize	*Visualise*
We're (we are)	*Were*
You're (you are)	*Your*

APPENDIX B — LIST OF CONTRIBUTORS

Certified Professional Members of *Career Professionals of Canada* are identified with the following credentials:

MCRS - Master Certified Résumé Strategist

MCIS - Master Certified Interview Strategist

MCES - Master Certified Employment Strategist

MCCS - Master Certified Career Strategist

CRS - Certified Résumé Strategist

CIS - Certified Interview Strategist

CES - Certified Employment Strategist

CCS - Certified Career Strategist

Sharon Graham, MCRS, MCIS, MCCS, MCES
Canada's Career Strategist
866-896-8768
www.sharongraham.ca
info@careerprocanada.ca

Career Professionals of Canada (Practitioners)
www.careerprocanada.ca

Career Professionals (Job Seekers and Workers)
www.careerprofessionals.ca

Paul Bennett
TARGET Career Services
604-876-9980, 888-7TARGET (782-7438)
www.choosetarget.com
info@choosetarget.com

Susan Kelly-Easton
Competitive Edge Career Services
250-964-1138, 888-964-1138
www.cecs.ca
newcareer@cecs.ca

Marian Bernard
The Regency Group
905-841-7120, 866-448-4672
www.resumeexpert.ca
marian@neptune.on.ca

Heather Erskine
Erskine Associates Inc.
519-642-1581
www.erskineassociates.com
heather.erskine@gmail.com

Skye Berry-Burke, CRS, CIS
Skye is the Limit Resume & Career Solutions
705-206-9988
www.skyeisthelimit.ca
info@skyeisthelimit.ca

Maureen Farmer, CRS
Word Right Career & HR Consulting
902-466-6661
www.wordrightresumes.com
maureen@wordrightresumes.com

Stephanie Clark
New Leaf Resumes
855-550-5627
www.newleafresumes.ca
newleafresumes@gmail.com

Howard Earle Halpern
Résu-Card ®
416-398-TALK (8255), 866-877-TALK (8255)
www.noblock.com
halpern@bellnet.ca

Brenda Collard-Mills, CRS
Robust Resumes and Resources
705-429-4073
www.robustresumesandresources.com
brenda@robustresumesandresources.com

Micheline Harvey
secretairevirtuelle.com
www.secretairevirtuelle.com
secretaire@secretairevirtuelle.com

155

APPENDIX B — LIST OF CONTRIBUTORS

François Houle
iWrite Business Services
www.iwritebusinessservices.com
career@iwritebusinessservices.com

Gabrielle LeClair, MCRS, MCIS, MCCS, MCES
GDL Consulting
www.linkedin.com/in/gabrielleleclair
gabrielleleclair@live.ca

Maureen McCann, MCRS, MCIS, MCCS, MCES
ProMotion Career Solutions
613-702-2122
www.mypromotion.ca
maureen@mypromotion.ca

Wayne Pagani, MCRS, MCIS, MCCS, MCES
W.P. Consulting & Associates
613-526-1982
www.developcareers.ca
developcareers@gmail.com

Lynda Reeves, MCRS
Added Value Résumés
addedvalueresumes@rogers.com

Pat Roberts, CRS
Georgian College
705-728-1968
www.georgianc.on.ca
pat.roberts@georgiancollege.ca

Linda Schnabel
CareerWorks
905-523-4281
www.careerworks.biz
info@careerworks.biz

Karen Shane, CRS
Business Writing & Resumes
416-226-0460
www.karenshane.ca
writinghelp@rogers.com

Karen Siwak, CRS
Resume Confidential
416-520-3772, 888-818-0079
www.resumeconfidential.ca
karen@resumeconfidential.ca

Marlene Slawson, CRS
Seneca College
416-491-5050
marlene.slawson@senecac.on.ca

Tanya Sinclair, CRS
TNT Human Resources Management
416-887-5819
info@tntresumewriter.com

Adrienne Tom, CRS
Career Impressions
587-332-6806
888-781-3056
www.careerimpressions.ca
info@careerimpressions.ca

Angelika Trinkwon, CRS
Angelika Trinkwon
250-713-7960
angelika@resumestrategist.ca

Mary Whitaker, CRS
Rite Careers
226-378-9301
www.ritecareers.com
mwhitaker@ritecareers.com

APPENDIX C — INDEX OF OBSTACLES

Nobody's perfect. Every candidate applying for a position brings many talents, skills, strengths, and achievements, but also areas that may considered obstacles. Strong cover letters de-emphasize personal challenges, issues with career history, or other areas that may be of concern to the reader.

Best Canadian Cover Letters provides many examples of ways to address common obstacles that you may encounter. You can find just a few examples here, but there are many more throughout the book:

Career Change
34, 39, 48, 68, 71, 81, 89, 91, 97, 109, 113, 141

Creating a Job
49, 115, 126, 136, 144, 145, 146, 147

Disability
43, 51, 94, 148, 149

Internal Position
72, 74, 80, 121

Experience Limited
36, 40, 47, 52, 54, 55, 56, 58, 62, 102

Career Gap
58, 60, 70, 83, 103

Limited Canadian Experience
37, 64, 73, 78, 83, 84, 101, 106, 119, 131, 132

Older Worker
45, 57, 65, 103, 124, 141

Relocating
50, 53, 79, 90, 98, 110, 138, 143

Moving Up
76, 112, 128, 137

The best way to deal with an obstacle is to avoid discussing it. So, if you have an obstacle that is not addressed in this list, it is likely that the writer has found a way to focus on the positives and eliminate the negatives from contention.

If you can't find an obstacle in one of our samples, you now know why it is a Best Canadian Cover Letter!

APPENDIX D — INDEX OF SAMPLES

APPENDIX D — INDEX OF SAMPLES

APPENDIX D — INDEX OF SAMPLES

ABOUT THE AUTHOR
Sharon Graham
Canada's Career Strategist
MCRS, MCIS, MCES, MCCS

Sharon Graham is Canada's Career Strategist. With a passion for career development, Sharon is committed to setting the standard for excellence in the industry. An outspoken advocate for ethics and integrity in the Canadian labour market, she has elevated procedures and practices within the sector.

In 2004, Sharon founded Career Professionals of Canada – an organization with a mandate to promote quality, ethics, and expertise within the industry. Recognized as an industry pioneer, Sharon championed the creation of a professional certification program to validate the expertise of résumé writers and other career professionals across the nation. She is also the force behind an Awards of Excellence program that recognizes practitioners who demonstrate the levels to which she aspires.

A firm believer in advancing the field, Sharon trains and mentors résumé writers and career practitioners across the nation. Through her books and other publications, she delivers cutting-edge innovations spanning strategic résumé writing, personal branding, employment consulting, and career development.

Having built one of Canada's most successful independent résumé writing and career transition firms for six-figure professionals, Sharon regularly acts in the capacity of a business consultant for practitioners who are operating small businesses. She generously shares her talents, business acumen, and best practices for starting and maintaining profitable operations.

Sharon Graham seeks to make a positive difference in every life she touches. It is her sincere wish that the strategies, information, and resources in this book will enable Canadians and others throughout the world to achieve their career goals.

Your success is Sharon's success!

Read Sharon Graham's Blog: http://www.SharonGraham.ca
Follow Sharon Graham on Twitter: http://twitter.com/sharongraham
Find Career Professionals: http://www.CareerProfessionals.ca
Join Career Professionals of Canada: http://wwwCareerProCanada.ca

Also by Sharon Graham
Canada's Career Strategist

Get Yours Today!

CareerProfessionals.ca
Resources for Job Seekers
www.CareerProfessionals.ca

Career Professionals of Canada
Association for Career Practitioners
www.CareerProCanada.ca